Defensive Tactics

Modern Arrest And Control Techniques
For Today's Police Warrior

by
Loren W. Christensen

Turtle Press   **Santa Fe, NM**

To contact the author or to order additional copies of this book:
    Turtle Press
    PO Box 34010
    Santa Fe NM 87594-4010
    1-800-77-TURTL
    www.TurtlePress.com

ISBN 978-1-880336-99-1
LCCN 2007049306
Printed in the United States of America

10 9 8 7 6 5 4 3 2

Library of Congress Cataloguing in Publication Data

Christensen, Loren W.
 Defensive tactics : modern arrest and control techniques for today's police warrior / by Loren W. Christensen. -- 1st ed.
    p. cm.
 ISBN 978-1-880336-99-1
 1. Police training. I. Title.
 HV7923.C53 2008
 363.2'3--dc22
                    2007049306

Defensive Tactics

Modern Arrest And Control Techniques

For Today's Police Warrior

Table of Contents

SECTION 9: TRAINING AND FIGHTING CONCEPTS   **363**

Acknowledgements

A big hug to my best friend, partner and love, Lisa Place. Thanks for the support

Pic taker:

Many thanks to Lisa Place for her patience behind the camera.

Posers:

Supermodels get paid thousands of dollars an hour. I pay my hard-working super models in burgers and fries. Many thanks to:

Lisa Place
Amy Widner
Jace Widmer
Dr. Dan Christensen
Rickie Place
Jericho Velasquez
Mark Mireles
Dave Tankersley
The tottering one is me

About the Author

Loren W. Christensen began his law enforcement career in 1967 as a military policeman in the army and then joined the Portland (Oregon) Police Bureau in 1972, retiring in 1997. During his years on the PPB, he worked street patrol, gang intelligence, dignitary protection, defensive tactics instructor, and riot control.

As a free-lance writer, Loren has authored over three dozen published books on a variety of subjects, dozens of magazine articles, and edited a newspaper for nearly eight years. He recently coauthored "The evolution of weaponry" with Lt. Col. Dave Grossman for the *Encyclopedia of Violence, Peace and Conflict* published by Academic Press. In 2007, Loren was accepted into the *The Heritage Registry of Who's Who* for "his accomplishments in the publishing industry."

Loren began training in the martial arts in 1965 and continues to this day. He has written over 20 books on the subject and has starred in six instructional DVDs. He has earned a total of 10 black belts, a 7th dan in karate, a 2nd dan in jujitsu, and a 1st dan in arnis.

Loren now writes full time and teaches martial arts to private students and a small group of regulars.

To contact Loren, visit his website LWC Books at : www.lwcbooks.com or www.lorenchristensen.com

It's always amazed me how few police officers train in the martial arts. Most love to shoot, rarely turning down an opportunity to plink holes in paper targets, but how often have you seen an officer pantomiming an armbar in the roll call room or two partners taking turns applying wristlocks in the fleet garage? Sometimes you see recruits in the academy practicing defensive tactics during their breaks, but mostly it's in preparation for an upcoming test. You hear them say enthusiastically that they want to perfect their tactics but that fades once they are assigned to a precinct.

I had about seven years of martial arts training under my belt when I joined the Portland Police Bureau, which included a year of practical fighting experience as an MP in Vietnam. The only other officer with martial arts experience was a judo black belt, the lone defensive tactics instructor. Over 1,100 officers and only two of us had martial arts training!

The fighting arts have been my life since 1965 so I often wonder why everyone doesn't practices this incredible lifestyle. Then I remember that I'm a bit of a fanatic. Even so, the police job puts officers into the toxic realm of the human condition, a place that is often as bad as it can get. So why wouldn't every officer want the additional edge that martial arts training gives? Beats me. Today, the fighting arts are more popular than ever and there are more officers training than there were a few years ago - but still not that many.

Another problem is that the number of defensive tactics instructors with a martial arts background is small. Usually what happens is that selected officers attend a two-week training seminar for certification to teach. I've only been to a couple of these as a trainer, so I can only guess that some are good and some aren't. Even when they are outstanding, the graduates have a limited knowledge of defensive tactics as a martial art. Can they teach a wristlock and an armbar? Sure. But the odds are high they might:

- leave something out.

- not know how to help an officer who can't apply a move properly when he is too short, too tall or too uncoordinated.

- not know when to change a pain technique to a leverage one.

- not understand the subtleties of balance.

- not understand the psychological/physiological link of different forms of distraction.

- not know how to block and shield.

- not know how to make a technique more effective.

- not know how to use various parts of the body as weapons.

- not understand the psychological/physiological link of blows to vulnerable targets.

- not know how to answer a host of "what if" questions.

I say this with complete respect for those officers who believe in defensive tactics enough to take the extra training (in some jurisdictions they do this on their own time and at their own expense) and then stand before the toughest audience in the world and impart what they know. Still, they don't know the answers to the above because as non martial artists, the knowledge isn't in their backgrounds. Nothing beats years of experience training, teaching and accumulating information.

The easy solution is for every police agency to use only veteran martial artists as their defensive tactics instructors. But that isn't going to happen because as mentioned, there aren't that many experts in police work. So it's up to those defensive tactics instructors who don't have a martial arts background to take it upon themselves to keep learning. If that's you, take every class you can, join a martial arts school that includes grappling in its offerings, research techniques on-line, buy books and DVDs. To use an apropos cliché: Knowledge is power.

In *Defensive Tactics*, I've drawn on my experience of 29 years in law enforcement, most of them as a defensive tactics instructor, and my training and teaching several martial arts styles to civilians since 1965. I've also received information, insight and help from many veteran martial arts friends, many of whom are in law enforcement now.

My objective here is to draw upon the martial arts to ensure that basic police defensive tactics techniques are done correctly and to show variations to enhance them so that you have a Plan B to transition to should the first variation not work well. I've also included principles and techniques that most police agencies don't incorporate into their program because of time limitations, budget issues, or because they don't know about them.

Police defensive tactics is a unique entity. It's not like full-contact taekwondo competition and mixed martial arts events where competitors do battle under rules that apply to both fighters. The law enforcement officer must follow rules established by city, state and federal laws, citizen demands, attorney demands, all with an objective of gaining control with minimum injury, while the violent suspect gets to follow that classic axiom: The only rule is that there aren't any.

Tough to do? You bet. It's just one more of a long list of hard tasks we ask you to do day in and day out.

I hope this book gives you an edge.

Author's Note

For ease of writing and reading, I have used the male gender "he" instead of the cumbersome "he/she." This is in no way intended to exclude the thousands of hard-working females patrolling our crime ridden streets everyday. Also, I have mostly used the word "police" for ease of writing and reading, with no disrespect intended to the many other types of law enforcement agencies.

The Foundation: Nuts and Bolts

While everyone wants to jump immediately into the punching, kicking, joint locks, and sleeper holds, it's critical to take the time to think about and understand the underpinning of defensive tactics. Consider this section as the cement foundation of the house. Without it, there isn't a lot of support for the walls, the beams and the ceiling. So that you don't end up under a pile of lumber, read this section first.

Thinking Ahead

It pays to plan ahead. It wasn't raining when Noah built the ark."
- Anon

Beside throwing each other down on the mats and wrenching arms beyond their intended range, it's valuable to prethink about engaging in a physical force situation. Here are a few subjects to ponder in your car as you cruise the hood on a slow, rainy Wednesday night.

Adrenaline Response

As we discuss accelerated heart rate and surging adrenaline, keep in mind that not everyone experiences these in a street scuffle or even in a shootout. You might experience them today but if you were to get into the same hairy situation tomorrow, you might not. Whenever this is discussed there is a risk of a self-fulfilling prophecy. You engage in a violent situation and, because you think you should be experiencing these things, you do. The idea is to understand that they can happen so they don't surprise you and affect your performance, while at the same time being cautious that knowing about the possibility doesn't make it happen.

Much of the following information is taken from *On Combat*, by Lt. Col. Dave Grossman and me, and from Bruce Siddle's *Sharpening the Warrior's Edge.*

Your ability to function deteriorates when your heart rate accelerates to around 175 bpm, though you're going to fare much better if you have trained to perform in this realm. Keep in mind that this type of rapid heart rate is caused by excitement, fear and a desperate need to survive. It's not the same as one accelerated from jogging or pumping on the Stairmaster. Here is the difference:

- An accelerated heart rate caused by exercise flushes your face (turns it red, if you're light skinned) as blood vessels dilate to allow blood to surge to your muscles.

- An accelerated heart rate caused by fear pales your face (turns it white, if you're light skinned) because of vasoconstriction, the narrowing of blood vessels that constricts or slows blood flow.

Should you run in desperation, adding physical exertion to your panic, your body will require additional fresh, oxygenated blood, just as your fear-induced vasoconstriction shuts down or constricts the vessels that deliver this much-needed supply. The result: an even higher heart rate.

FACT   Your heart rate can go from 70 bpm to 220 bpm in less than half a second.

Let's take a quick look at the stages of an accelerated heart rate, data based on an article by researchers Bruce Siddle and Dr. Hal Breedlove entitled "Survival Stress Reaction" and from Siddle's excellent book Sharpening the Warrior's Edge: The Psychology and Science of Training. When we talk about fear-induced accelerated heart rate, we're talking about Survival Stress Reaction (SSR).

- Around 115 bpm, most people lose fine motor skills, such as finger dexterity and eye-hand coordination, making it virtually impossible to, say, type in a code to unlock a door or find the right key in a cluster of keys. Multitasking also becomes difficult.

- Around 145 bpm, most people lose their complex motor skills, movements that involve a series of muscle groups, such as eye-hand coordination, precise tracking of movement, and exact timing. Executing complicated self-defense techniques becomes difficult if not impossible.

- Around 175 bpm, most people experience numerous negative effects: tunnel vision (meaning a loss of depth perception) and loss of memory of what happened (though there is usually a 30 percent recall after the first 24 hours, 50 percent after two days, and 75 to 95 percent after three to four days).

- At 185–220 bpm, most people go into a state of "hypervigilance," sometimes referred to as the "deer in the headlights" mode. This is often characterized by performing actions that are useless, such as continuing to desperately twist a doorknob on a locked door. People in this condition are often unable to move or scream. When they do move, they sometimes do so irrationally by leaving their place of cover.

Trained people have an advantage. Your Survival Stress Reaction (SSR), whether it's in the 115 bpm range or 220, happens without conscious thought. Siddle and other researchers of SSR tested police officers and soldiers, people in high-risk jobs who engage in considerable training that is far greater in quantity and sophistication than what the average person gets who works in an office or warehouse. Their research has found that a trained person can function with an accelerated heart rate of 115 to 145 bpm and, when it climbs higher, a trained person can lower it consciously to within that workable area.

Along with training in an environment that teaches you to function under stress, you also benefit from correct breathing. Sure, you do that quite well now, but let's examine a powerful technique that will amaze you at how quickly it brings on physical and mental calm.

The Power Of Combat Breathing

Four-count breathing is a highly effective and easy-to-do technique that slows your thumping heartbeat, reduces the tremble in your hands, clears your mind, and envelopes you in a sense of calm and control. Although this powerful tool has been used in the martial arts, yoga, and medical field for a long time, it's only been in recent years that it has been popularized in the military and law enforcement communities by Lt. Col. Dave Grossman (*On Combat*) and others.

The technical term for the procedure is autogenic breathing, but police officers and soldiers call it tactical breathing or combat breathing. SWAT officers report that they have used it just before making a high-risk forced entry. Soldiers use it to bring calm to their minds and bodies before they go into battle, and again after the battle to "come down" from the adrenaline rush. High school and college students are finding that it reduces test anxiety, and many surgeons use it before beginning a delicate operating procedure where optimum fine motor control is needed.

How to do it

Begin by breathing in through your nose to a slow count of four, feeling your lower belly expand. Hold for a slow count of four, and then slowly exhale through your lips for a count of four, letting your belly deflate. Hold empty for a slow count of four and then repeat the process. Here is the entire procedure:

- Breathe in through your nose two, three, four. Hold two, three, four.

- Exhale out through your lips two, three, four. Hold two, three, four.

- Breathe in through your nose deep, deep, deep. Hold two, three, four.

- Exhale out through your lips two, three, four. Hold two, three, four.

- Breathe in through your nose two, three, four. Hold two, three, four.

- Exhale out through your lips two, three, four. Hold two, three, four.

That's it. Simple. You don't need to sit before a candle or burn incense. Do it anywhere and anytime (I've done it while jammed in a police van with several other cops, racing through predawn streets on the way to a high-risk raid on a gangster house. And no one was aware I was doing it). The beauty of this wonderful tool is that you can adapt it easily to your needs. Most people find that the described three-cycle procedure works well to bring calm to their minds and bodies. But you might need four to six cycles to get the benefits. If you want to hold each count for five seconds rather than four, do it. It's about making it work for you. Don't wait until you're in the middle of a dangerous situation to experiment. Practice this breathing procedure once or twice a day to learn what method works best for you (and to award yourself with a few moments of calm and clarity). Practice now so that it will be there for you when you need it most.

The Importance Of Visualizing

I've written about visualization, AKA: mental imagery, for years in magazine articles and books because I'm convinced it's one of the most powerful training devices we have available to us. One writer said this about it: "Visualization is important because it makes the future become clear. Seeing yourself already achieving your goal makes your brain believe that attaining that goal is possible." In addition, consistently imagining a goal, or a skill set, helps you attain it much faster. Now, here is the real good news: You can do it in your pajamas, in your swim trunks, and in your police uniform. You can do it your easy chair, lying in a hammock, or sitting in your squad watching traffic. The only "equipment" you need is your imagination.

This is how easy it is. Pick up a mug shot and look at the bozo's face. Now put it down and try to remember what he looked like. If you see a face that looks anything like the person, you're visualizing. If you don't, try this. Look at the picture for a few seconds and then close your eyes. Open them again and look at it, then close them again. Open, close, open, close. Do this for a few minutes. When you can see the picture but you don't know whether your eyes are open or closed – you're on your way to visualization skill. The more you practice this the better you get at it.

Now, park your car across the street from the convenience store at Broadway and Main. Look at those two guys standing on the corner, smoking and laughing. Close your eyes, open your eyes and look at them, close your eyes, open your eyes and look at them, and so on. Do this about ten times. Once you can see them – standing near the store's big window with that butcher paper sign advertising beer, with the dumpster alongside the building, the fire hydrant at the corner, the parking lot on the east side, and the door at the front – and you don't know if your eyes are open or closed, you're ready to do some serious visualizing that will help your performance in a high-risk situation.

You're going to see yourself confronting these two. Here are three easy tips before you start:

• See the action out of your eyes, as opposed to watching it as if looking at a movie.

• Fill the whole "screen" in your mind's eye, all in vivid color and surround sound.

• Visualize in real-time, that is, at the same speed the real action would occur.

Visualize the confrontation

- As you imagine walking up to the men, see them look at you.

- See yourself stop outside of their arm's reach.

- Feel your body stand at an angle, see and feel your hands lift up in front of you to gesture, and hear your voice ask them for identification.

- See one of them reach into his pocket for his wallet.

- See and hear the other person become agitated and demand why you are harassing them.

- Feel the fight or flight juices surge through your body, as you become hypervigilant.

- Feel your heart rate surge as you see the agitated man throw a punch at you.

- See and feel your arm snap up to protect your head.

- Feel and hear his hand hit your arm and jar your head.

- See your arms snap out and feel your body launch into him...

- ...and so on.

This is an incredibly powerful tool used more and more by Olympic athletes, the military, martial artists and law enforcement. There is nothing terribly mysterious about it, or supernatural, it's simply a powerful mental tool that allows you to rehearse a physical response. In the end, your mind and body acts as if you physically practiced your block and follow-up.

FAST REPS

A real situation can deteriorate and turn physical in 10 seconds. Therefore, when you imagine a suspect attacking you and you imagine your response – your favorite move or any technique in this book – for one minute, that is enough time for you to practice four or five visualized "reps." Do it for five minutes and you can easily get in 20 reps or more. Pretty good deal and you don't wrinkle or sweat-stink your clothes. Practice five minutes or longer three or four times a week.

The Value of Reps: More Training in Less Time

As long as I can remember, students have asked me what the "The Secret" is that will make them faster, stronger, more flexible, and a better fighter. So is there a secret to acquiring skill in the combat arts? Yes. The secret is …train hard.

I know, I know. That's not a secret and it's not even mystical. Sorry, but training hard is the only way to get good. There are no short cuts, no easy paths, and no special meditations.

Still, too many people waste precious time looking for a quick and easy path to combat effectiveness. I call them the McDonald's Generation, people used to driving up to a window to get an instant meal. But not everything can be gotten as easily as that. Some things you have to work for - like physical skill.

It's All About Reps

Within the first so-called secret is the concept of repetition. It takes many reps to polish a technique and to ingrain it into the brain so that it's there for you when things get ugly. There is an old saying in the martial arts: "It's better to do 10 correct repetitions than 100 poor ones." I disagree. I tell my students that it's better to do 500 correct ones than 10 good ones.

Repetition practice works well on the firing range. Every time you fire a box of ammo, you get in 50 reps of gripping, sight alignment, trigger pull, and so on. When you spend an afternoon shooting, you might do hundreds of reps; spend a week at the range and you knock out thousands. In time, the movements become second nature, which is exactly what you want them to be when the you-know-what hits the fan and you have to shoot fast and accurately.

When you do it correctly and do it in volume, repetition practice in defensive tactics provides the same benefits. Unfortunately, it's the critical element missing from many programs, mostly because of time contraints. What you need is a way to squeeze in lots of reps in an ever-shrinking time allotment for DT training, and do so in a way to keep the students, many of whom would rather be doing something else, interested and progressing.

Let's look at two training methods that allow you to experience a variety of approaches and a variety of training partners. One method uses that old standard commonly called the "Line Drill" and the other uses what martial artists call, "Monkey Line Drill."

Line Drill: Attack And Response

The instructor divides the class in half and has the students form two lines, Line A officers facing Line B officers. Line A is the attacker and Line B the observer and defender. You're in Line B. For discussion purposes, let's keep the attackers' move easy; they simply extend their arms – it can be a punch or a push - toward your line. The drill is to break the attack into phases then practice each repetitiously

Your line faces the attackers as if interviewing them on the street: standing at an angle, feet staggered, and hands up. As the suspects reach forward with their right hands to shove or punch, your line will:

• Phase 1: observe the attack.

• Phase 2: swat it aside in the direction of the suspect's other arm.

• Phase 3: step toward the attacker's right side and then grab their right upper arm and wrist. Then they turn the rest of the way so that each officer in your line faces the same direction as their respective attacker faces.

While the attackers' action might justify a greater response than what I'm describing here, let's keep it simple for the sake of this discussion. The final position in the last bullet is commonly called "The Minimum Custody Hold" (shown in many of the techniques throughout this book), which is used to walk a nonviolent suspect a short distance and a position from which you can execute several pain compliance holds and takedowns.

Here are the three phases:

Phase 1: Training your eye

On the instructor's count, Line A attacks the officers in Line B by thrusting their hands toward them. Here is where we depart from the usual way of responding. You and everyone else in Line B only watch the thrust.

This phase is for you to observe and only observe how an attacker moves as he reaches or punches his arm forward. Note where his eyes look, how his shoulders move, the way in which his hand and arm move forward, and how his body and feet move. This phase "educates" your eyes to recognize all the subtle and not so subtle movements that initiate an aggressive straight-line thrust of the hand. The ultimate objective of the exercise is for officers to react more quickly to this specific threat by virtue of recognizing and understanding all the little movements that make up the big movement.

Both lines should act as the attacker for 20 reps with each hand while the other line carefully observes and studies the movements.

SUPERNATURAL?

Many stories tell of great martial arts masters who supposedly knew telepathically when and how an attacker was going to attack. Nonsense. There was nothing mystical about their ability other than they were extremely adept at perceiving even the minutest movements that preceded the larger attack motion. Those masters knew, as many of today's experts know, all the subtle movements that precede an attack, whether it's straight-line, circular, diagonal, upward or downward, and whether it's a punch, kick, or an attack with a weapon. You can, too, with hard training and many reps.

Phase 2: Swatting

In this phase your line swats the thrust aside. When the instructor counts aloud, Line A thrusts their hands forward and Line B, who is standing in an interview position with their left sides angled forward, swats the attack aside with their left hands. Your swat should be short and quick, with no extension or wasted motion (see Chapter 5). The block is all that occurs at this phase. If this is a new exercise, the instructor should have everyone practice the moves slowly.

Both lines should act as the attacker for 20 reps with each hand while the other line carefully observes the thrust and blocks.

Phase 3: Two-Handed Grab

As the instructor counts, Line A thrusts their hands toward Line B. Swat the hand away as you did before, then step forward slightly with your lead foot, grasp the attacker's upper arm with your left hand and his wrist with your right, and then turn to face in the same direction as your attacker (see Chapter 4). Now you're in a position to escort a cooperative person a short distance or execute any number of handcuffing techniques, control holds, and takedowns.

Both lines should act as the attacker for 20 reps with each hand while the other line carefully observes the thrust, blocks it, and then steps in to secure the attacker's arm.

This 3-phase exercise gives you 60 reps with each arm for a total of 120 reps. Since the attacker is getting to watch the officer practice 120 moves, and the officer is getting to watch the attacker's body mechanics as he executes 120 hands thrusts, both benefit from hundreds of reps. Not a bad deal for an exercise that takes no longer than 15 minutes to complete and one that holds students' interest.

At the conclusion of each 3-phase exercise, everyone moves to the right and repeats the exercise with a new partner, or the class can begin a new drill.

Later in the same training session or when the class meets again, the instructor can combine the elements of the technique into one smooth movement or, if he feels everyone needs extra practice on a particular step, he can again break it into three phases. When he feels the students are ready to add a pain compliance hold, say a wristlock, he can add it on as a fourth phase. If it's a new wristlock, he can break it into two moves, a phase 4 and a phase 5.

Monkey Line Drill

In the Monkey Line Drill, you face a column of student attackers who face you. One at a time, each one steps up and launches an attack to which you respond with whatever the exercise calls for. The attacker then moves to the end of the column and the next one advances to attack.

I've used the Monkey Line Drill in police defensive tactics classes for years, relying on its versatility and enjoying the benefits my students get. One of its many attributes is that it allows you to practice a technique - an entire move or just part of one - on several students of varying physique types: short, tall, heavy, slight, male, female, long-armed, short-armed, flexible, and stiff. Use it to work just about any DT drill as long as there are at least five or six students. If there are 20 students, form two or three monkey lines.

The greater the number of opponents you can train with, the greater your understanding of the large and small intricacies of a technique. In addition, if you only change opponents once or twice during a class, it would take several classes to give you this broad experience. But in the time it takes you to go through the Monkey Line Drill just once – two or three minutes - you experience training with 10 people of various sizes and shapes. Take another trip through and you will have practiced 20 repetitions with 10 opponents in less than 10 minutes. That is an excellent use of training time.

Let's revisit the same one-hand thrust we discussed in the Line Drill. Counting you, there are 11 students in the class and you've been chosen to be "it" first. Stand in place and wait as the others form a column facing you. Let's begin with Phase 1.

Phase 1: Training your eye

Some officers might not take this phase seriously so allow me to discuss its merits a little more. An inadequately trained officer won't see a suspect's fist until *after* it's rushing toward his face. Of course, that's better than not seeing the fist at all since there might be a chance to duck or block it. But it's chancy, especially if the officer is having an off day or the suspect is having an especially good one. An officer should be able to read the danger signals long before the fist reaches his jaw.

Consider this scenario: An officer stops a man on the street to check his ID. The guy becomes agitated, displaying the usual indignation shtick and chanting the "This is harassment" mantra. Then, *without forewarning*, he punches the officer's face.

Wait. Did he really launch his fist without forewarning? No. It's impossible to do. It was there, but the officer simply didn't recognize it.

Punches, kicks, pushes, tackles, and any other attack are telegraphed by first moving the shoulders, head, chest, or entire torso. The assailant might also telegraph by twitching his mouth, inhaling or exhaling sharply, leaning his upper body forward, and clenching and unclenching his fists. Even highly trained fighters and thugs who have "trained" on the streets do these things, but with such subtlety or so quickly the movements are virtually imperceptible. Untrained people, who thankfully you deal with the most, telegraph with all the subtly of beating on a base drum. The Monkey Line Drill is an especially valuable tool to help you experience these pre-launch movements.

Stand in front of a column of fellow students in your standard interview position as if you were dealing with a routine, low-level threat on the street. The first attacker steps close enough to strike you in the face. At this point, he can thrust his hand all the way out as was done in the Line Drill, or he can do what I call "the origin of movement."

Origin of movement As you carefully analyze your attacker, he extends his arm as if to punch, but only a few inches, about one quarter or less of the distance toward your face. Your job is to watch everything that moves at the launch point: his shoulder, head, mouth, chest, and his opposite arm. He then goes to the rear of the column and the next student steps forward to execute a partial thrust. Continue until you have gone through everyone in the line. Then it's someone else's turn.

Phase 2: Swatting

To practice the swat block, stand in your interview position facing the column of attackers. As each attacker steps up to you and thrusts his hand out, swat the attack aside with your closest hand. The swat is short and quick, with no extension or wasted motion. That attacking student moves to the back of the column and then the next one moves up.

The swat block is all that occurs in this phase.

Phase 3: Two-Handed Grab

As you face the column in your interview stance, the first student moves into range and thrusts out his hand. Sweep it aside. Then step forward with your lead foot as you grasp the attacker's upper arm with your left hand and his wrist with your right. Turn your body so that you're in a position to escort him a short distance, handcuff him, or apply a control hold. That attacker then moves to the end of the column and the next one moves up to thrust his hand at you.

The instructor can modify the Line Drill and the Monkey Line Drill as needed:

- If most students have trouble with, say, the swat block phase, the instructor can repeat it until the students can execute it flawlessly.

- If the class consists of new and advanced students, the instructor can form a Monkey Line for each group.

- The instructor can have the attackers go slowly the first time through and increase the speed as everyone progresses.

- The instructor can easily determine when the class is ready to do a technique in its entirety and when certain individuals need more phase training.

Both formats are excellent training devices that:

- condense training time.

- allow students to practice against a variety of people.

- provide instructors with greater visibility and control of large classes.

- accelerate learning when used in conjunction with phase training.

Instructors should use their imaginations to find more ways to use these line drills.

The Elements of Balance

When you control the suspect's balance, you control the suspect, and yourself. Conversely, when you don't control his balance, you're probably not controlling yours and you're both likely to kiss the sidewalk. Balance is critical when dealing with a resistor, so critical that if you don't have it, all the defensive tactics techniques in the world aren't going to help you. It's true in shooting and it's true when it's hands-on time with someone.

Let's look at a simple concept that when understood will help keep your balance stable and the arrested suspect at your mercy.

The Tripod Concept

A camera needs a three-legged stand, a tripod. If it has only two legs, the stand and the camera will fall over. You have only two legs but you don't fall over because you have equilibrium. Knock back five too many beers, however, and you obliterate your balance to the extent that you become that two-legged tripod in search of support.

Your equilibrium is on the job 24/7 sending your body little and big adjustments to keep you upright. Nonetheless, know that your balance is weakest in the direction of that invisible third leg.

The invisible third leg

The circles indicate where the 3rd leg would be, and where you're weak.

Your balance is weak to the front and rear.

When your feet are in alignment, your balance is weak to each side.

No matter how you configure your legs, your balance is weak where that third tripod leg would be if you didn't have equilibrium.

Be cognizant of how you stand when talking to one or more suspects. They likely won't know the tripod concept, but a lucky push can send you down anyway.

Stance not staggered

A full facing stance makes you vulnerable... ...to a straight on push.

Staggered stance

You're standing in a staggered stance talking to a dangerous suspect.

Should he surprise you with a straight-on shove, it might knock you back a little, but a staggered stance provides you with a better chance of staying in balance.

How not to face two suspects

You're facing one suspect in a strong, angled stance but your vulnerable invisible third leg side is exposed to her friend.

He pushes you.

A better way

Point your lead foot between the two suspects.

How not to stand when handcuffing

Look at the previous pics of the circles on the ground. Where are the weak points?

Here is the answer.

A better way

Stand at an angle.
Should he push you,
your stability helps you resist.

Be cognizant as to how you're standing when applying a control hold. When you can't help but use a vulnerable stance, you should at least know that you're doing so.

You're still vulnerable

An accidental lucky push, or one done by someone who has knowledge of balance, can still knock you over if you're not cognizant. Here is an example.

You're standing in a staggered stance, a strong position as you face him.

He suddenly steps to your front, turns and pushes toward your invisible support leg.

Be cognizant of your position

Order the suspect to stand fast while you talk to him.

Should he move in either direction, continue to command him to stand still as you turn with him.

Using the tripod to your advantage

Once you understand the simple tripod concept, you're going to see many opportunities to apply it. The only caveat to the following technique examples, and with others you find on your own, is that you must execute the moves fast. Should you move too slowly, the suspect might brace himself. Seek that moment when he is at his most vulnerable, then explode.

Clinch

You're in a clinch and dancing about with a suspect you're arresting.

At the exact moment he spreads his feet, reach for the back of his head and pull it forcefully downward in the direction where his support leg would be.

Try to angle him so that he reaches to brace himself, thus putting that arm out of commission. Use whatever control hold you want to force him into the prone.

SENSITIVITY DRILL

This is a fun drill that develops awareness of your opponent's balance. There are many variations; here are two to begin with. Consider them Stage 1 and Stage 2.

Stage 1: Clinch with your training partner using any technique you've studied from a martial art system, from high school wrestling, or just latch onto each other's shirts as so often happens in the street. Jostle about – pulling, pushing, and turning – as you strive to get a sense of your opponent's balance. *Feel* his weight shift from left to right and from right to left. *Feel* him lean forward and feel him lean back. Don't try to resist or encourage his shifting balance. Just learn how it *feels*.

Stage 2: You and your training partner do the same drill as just described, but when you feel his balance shift in a given direction, give him a nudge. For example, when his weight shifts toward you, pull him a little by his shirt, arm, neck or whatever you're grasping. Don't turn this into a competitive muscle contest. The objective is to develop sensitivity to another person's balance.

Arm pull forward

You've grabbed the suspect's arm to take him into custody but he suddenly twists toward you. His weight is centered or leaning slightly toward you.

Forcefully yank his arm downward in the direction where is support leg would be.

- **Don't** pull his arm too far forward.

- **Do** pull it about 12 inches or so in front and between his feet.

- **Don't** pull the suspect's arm down and in front of one of his legs, which leaves him balanced and strong.

- **Do** pull it forward and between his feet.

Arm pull back

You grab the suspect's arm to take him into custody but he twists toward you. His weight is centered or back a little.

Step forward and to the suspect's side. Using your body weight, yank his arm down in the direction of where his tripod leg would rest. Make sure to pull it between his feet and about a foot or so out from his heels.

Keep hold of his arm as he lands so that he doesn't fall on it (which could be injurious) and so that you can keep control of it. Immediately execute a rollover technique to get him on his belly.

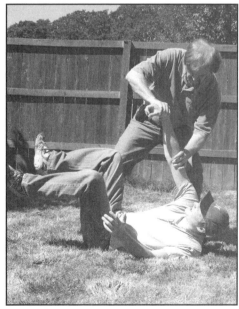

Warning: Be cautious of where you execute the "arm pull back" so that he lands safely. Landing on curbs, stairs and other hard objects could cause unintended injury.

Upper chest press takedown

This technique is a tad more difficult than the last three but well worth the practice time. When done right, it looks effortless since it's not about muscle, but rather an understanding of the suspect's vulnerable tripod leg.

You grab the suspect's right arm to take him into custody but he stiffens. You decide to take him down.

Step into him with your left leg behind his knee and shoot your left arm across his chest. Notice your angle to him.

Press his chest and simultaneously pop his knee. Down he goes. (left)

Although it's called the "upper-chest press," you can also press his face. (above)

Kuzushi

Kuzushi (pronounced koo zoo she) is a Japanese word that comes from the verb kuzureru, meaning "to break or crumble." For purposes of police work, it means "unbalance." I'll use both terms as we proceed just because it's fun to say kuzushi from time to time.

Although most police defensive tactics involve unbalancing, most often officers learn the mechanics of techniques without ever hearing the word "unbalance" (let alone kuzushi). However, by understanding this powerful but simple principle, your techniques take on a greater clarity so that you can answer many of your own "what if" questions.

Kuzushi made easy

Standing straight and tall, this man is relatively difficult to move off balance.

But when he is leaning forward, back or to the side, he is in a state of unbalance.

Even a slight nudge against an already unbalanced person will "crumble" his foundation.

Don't fight against it

When an officer doesn't understand the significance of balance, he often errs by fighting against it.

Clinch:

You're tussling with the suspect who leans forward about 45 degrees.

Don't try to push his chin up and back to dump him onto his back.

Do take him in the direction that he is already off balance. Slip your arm onto the back of his head and press down.

Armbar takedown:

You're trying to take the suspect down with an armbar to your right...

...when he manages to resist by pulling the other way.

Don't fight his pull because you might lose.

Do go with his pull and add your energy to his.

Take away his strength by taking away his balance

Handcuffing:

Don't allow the suspect to be in balance during handcuffing.

Do take him off balance to reduce his ability to resist.

Come-a-long hold:

Don't apply a weak wristlock as it allows the suspect to stay in balance.

Do apply sufficient pressure to force him up onto his toes to weaken his balance.

Takedown

This common leg sweep technique is often taught without emphasizing the importance of unbalancing the suspect first.

Leg sweep:

Don't attempt the leg sweep while the suspect is still standing straight up and in balance.

Do pull the suspect's arm downward, press up on his chin, and position your outside foot at an outward angle to unbalance him and prevent his resistance...

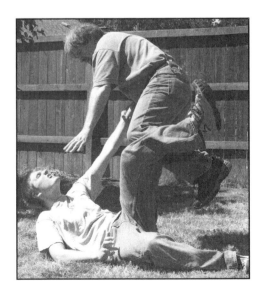

...so that your leg sweep goes smoothly.

Lunge:

Don't resist his forward momentum as he charges off the stool.

Do step aside and assist him in the direction he is off balance.

Mental Kuzushi

Disrupting his mental balance works wonders, too. You probably have used verbal and physical techniques for a long time, although you haven't attached the word kuzushi to them.

Words to distract

Here are three verbal techniques that usually (meaning: not always) worked for me when I needed to distract a suspect for a second so I could move in on him:

"Is that your car over there?"

"Do you know that guy across the street?"

The one that never failed: "Do you know that hooker's name?"

Up until I asked one of these questions, the suspect's full attention was on me: trying to read my intention; seeing if I believed his lies; looking for a weakness in my attention. My question unbalanced his focus for a brief moment, similar to the way a karate yell works, allowing me a small window of opportunity to step in and grab him.

Words to slow the suspect's thinking

This old technique is still an effective one to buy a second in which to move against a weapon. It involves getting the suspect to speak or to listen – then you move.

When he is listening to you speak – hearing the words, deciphering their meaning, mulling a response – and you suddenly lunge toward him, he has to stop his mental process to put into play another mental process: his response. Or, when he is talking – thinking about his words, formulating his sentences, wondering if he is convincing you – and you suddenly lunge toward him, he has to stop speaking and put into play a mental process as to how to respond.

Which is better? I've used both and found that when he is speaking I get two hairs of a second longer to move. But that's just my experience. I don't know of any studies that show one being preferable to the other.

Drop something of his

This technique is a combination mental and physical kuzushi. He is happy in his mind that things are going well and then you take that away from him.

Say you've got the suspect's driver's license and ran a check for warrants. Dispatch says he has two. The guy didn't hear that information but he is still getting twitchy. So you talk to him for a few seconds as if all is well.

"Thanks, My Widmer," you say, handing his license to him. You let go of it too soon. It either flutters to the ground and the suspect bends off balanced to retrieve it, or you release it close enough so that he lunges for it, placing him off balance.

You immediately take advantage of his mental and physical unbalance and lunge for his arm to apply a control hold.

A Fun Exercise

Whenever you're sitting in your police car watching sidewalk traffic, or walking your beat, or even when you're off duty and standing in line at the movies or the grocery, watch people as to how they move and stand.

- A man by the streetlight stands with his feet spread slightly, his weight equally distributed on both feet, and his arms folded.

- A woman leans against a bus stop shelter, much of her weight on her left leg.

- A teen gets up from the bus stop bench by leaning his weight forward and then straightening.

- As a woman walks down a set of stairs, note how one foot hangs in the air for just a moment.

First, just study these people to see how they distribute their weight and how they are off balance at various times, even if for just for a second.

Then think how you would "encourage" each person to remain off balance: a nudge, a hard push, a trip, a bop on the back of the head, or a sophisticated technique.

Developing self-awareness

The next phase of the exercise is to recognize when you are off balance. On an average day of walking, sitting, standing, getting up, getting down, turning, pushing and pulling, you're off balance hundreds of times, maybe more. While most often you can't help this, you can develop an instinct for knowing when it happens. The old axiom "knowledge is power" goes a long way toward helping you to be cognizant of your balance.

This is especially true when dealing with a threatening suspect. We know that we shouldn't expose our gun side. We know that we shouldn't step within arm's reach of the suspect if we're not physically arresting him. We know that we should give ourselves a safety zone when making a car stop. Nonetheless, these critical rules get violated because of circumstances beyond our control. When they do, and they can't be fixed, we must be aware of the fact that it's happening and perform accordingly.

Crossing the Gap

Moving into Range

A potentially dangerous moment

Martial artists train hard so that they can cross that empty space - that hot zone – between themselves and the adversary. A fighter can have the best punches and kicks this side of Bruce Lee but if he can't cross that space without getting clobbered, his super techniques are for naught.

I did an informal survey at my agency one year and found that most of the minor and major assaults on officers happened when they moved in to apply hands on. It just makes sense when you think about what it means to the bad guy. He knows that your advance means that his freedom to walk wherever he wants, to buy a burger, and to steal, rape and burn is about to be taken away from him. Up until you moved toward him, he thought he was doing a good job lying to you. But when he sees your body incline in his direction and your foot move in his direction, he knows the jig is up. Sometimes he simply exhales his resignation and offers no resistance, while other times his sudden realization makes him reflexively or purposely stiffen, turn to run, flail his arms, or smash you in the nose.

His body language

Sometimes a suspect clearly verbalizes his message that he is going to resist: "Touch me and I'll kill you," "You better get more cops," "I'm not going to let you arrest me." Other suspects won't comment verbally, though they display certain signals with their body that indicate their intention. For example:

Face:

- A sudden change from his wide-eyed and lifted-eyebrows look of fake innocence to bunched eyebrows, narrowed eyes and overall facial tension, as if his skin is suddenly too small for his skull.

- Sudden tightening of the lips.

- A facial tick.

- Eyes appearing to go out of focus or they narrow, as he looks off to the side and appears to be in a trance. I call this the "German shepherd stare" because it's a trait dogs do just before they rip into your inner, upper tender thigh.

Body

- Twitching (ants in the pants), feet shuffling, head turning this way and that way.

- Hands hanging at his sides, repeatedly closing into fists and opening again.

- He initially faces you straight on during your contact, but he turns himself into a quarter turn (the same position you should be using). Although not every resistor is going to shift into this position, those who do are often trained fighters, either "trained" through street experience or trained via formal classes.

Your stance

As always, you should be in your interview stance, hands up and open. Now, don't hold your arms stiff and motionless because it looks weird and it's easy for the suspect to see when you move. Even if you don't talk with your hands much, start. You might feel like a bad actor at first but that will pass. When it does, you're left with a subtle device that camouflages your intention. Then when you do move to grab him, it takes a moment longer for it to register in his brain that you're not just gesturing again. Here are a couple of bumper stickers:

Action from non-action is easy to see

Action from action is harder to see

Timing the move

Throughout this book, I suggest moving in on the suspect whenever you have a window of opportunity. Here is a list of a few typical moments. Since the window is open only briefly, you have to move fast.

- The suspect is distracted by a passing vehicle.

- The suspect looks toward his buddy.

- The suspect looks over as your backup arrives.

- You sucker him into looking, by asking, "You know that guy?" Is that your car?"

- You deliberately drop his license.

- You ask for his identification.

- You ask him to step up onto the curb.

- You ask him a hard question.

All of the above are based on the principle that a person can think of only one thing at a time. The moment his thinking process changes - you move.

Where to move

When possible, move in at an angle to his right side.

Gesture with your finger tips, your hand at the same level as his face. This small gesture forces him to look at your fingers (and also positions your arm and hand where it can protect your face) which buys you a second or two to step in...

...to secure his right arm. According to different studies, 85 to 90 percent of the population is right handed. Secure his right hand to negate a little of his strength and coordination. Don't stop in front of him where he can hit you. Move to his side as shown.

How to grab

Unless the guy is resisting, or you sense that he is about to, don't grab his arm so hard you squeeze all the juice out of his flesh. If he wasn't combative before, he probably will be now. Instead, grab him firmly and authoritatively. He knows you're in charge without crushing his bones.

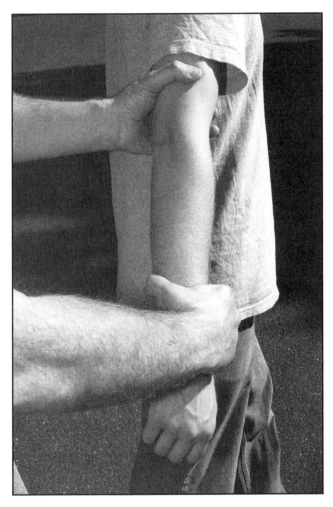

Grip one hand just above his elbow, your other on his wrist. Because your thumbs point in opposite directions, your hold isn't easily defeated.

How to move the suspect before he's handcuffed

You walk him; don't let him walk you. Ensure that he doesn't lag behind a step or surge forward a step. Both positions are weak ones for you.

Should he balk a little, solidify his wrist and push more forcefully on his elbow. Lower your body a little so that you draw on the power of your legs to drive him forward.

Blocking

In whatever setting I've taught over the years, whether law enforcement or private citizens, students are always anxious to practice the fun stuff – punches, kicks, throws, joint locks – missing the glaring fact that if an attacker hits them first they might not get a chance to do the fun stuff.

When you're on the receiving end of an incoming foot, fist, or a 2 x4 board, it's critical that your defense is a simple one based on natural reaction. Toss a Nerf ball at a child when he doesn't expect it and his hand snaps up to swat it aside, or he lifts his arm to cover his head. That natural response is what we want to use and polish.

Blocking and Shielding

Technically this is a deflection rather than a block. The punch or push enters your space and you swat it aside as if it's an annoying mosquito. Don't glom onto the suspect's arm and don't push it farther away than is necessary. Simply swat it off its course and snap your arm back, or launch a counter grab or hit.

Let's look at a few simple blocks that are based on natural reflexes.

Swat to the inside

From your hands-up stance...

...swat your lead hand from in front of its shoulder...

...across your body and to the front of your other shoulder. There is no need to go farther since you don't exist beyond that point and doing so would leave you too exposed. Keep your other hand up so it's available for blocking or countering.

Swat to the outside

From your hands-up stance...

...swat the back of your hand from the center of your body...

...to an inch or two outside your shoulder. Then snap it back to the starting place or proceed with a counter. Keep your other hand up and ready to use.

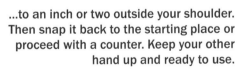

Shielding

This is a favorite among boxers and mixed martial artists. They favor it over any other block because they don't have to commit their arm to swat away an attack. So why shouldn't we use it all the time? Because it really hurts! A full-contact fighter hits his opponent's bare arms with relatively cushy gloves, and even that hurts. Being hit with bare knuckles hurts much more and could, because of the many sensitive nerves therein, debilitate the arm.

While shielding is an excellent block, I suggest using it as a last resort. I call it an "Eeek! block" because the attacker strikes out so quickly or suddenly that your only option is to take the blow on a limb to shield a precious target, such as your face or ribs.

Head shield

From your hands-up stance, raise your arm to shield the side of your head. Make sure to press your arm against it. You don't want your unsupported arm struck and then driven into your skull.

Press both arms against your head when defending against a suspect flailing with both of his fists.

Body shield

Squish your upper body down and press your forearm against your side.

Shield with both arms when the suspect flails.

Incorporate blocking into your training as you work on other material throughout this book. Block your training partner's punch or push, and then either step back and retrieve one of your belt weapons, or lunge forward with a counter hit or grappling move. Make blocking part of your regular training so that it's there for you when you need it.

Weight Training and Aerobics

Here is something I've observed since the mid 1960s when I began teaching cops and civilians how to defend themselves: cops and martial artists who lift weights and do aerobic activities are better at defensive tactics and martial arts than those who don't. I'm guessing that it's their body awareness that helps them catch on to the teaching faster and executing the techniques more easily.

That said, sometimes a weight lifter, especially a hardcore bodybuilder, thinks too much about his exterior to the extent he over-muscles techniques. After all, that is how he lifts, that is what makes the barbell go up and come back down with control. But once he learns not to flex when doing defensive tactics, not to care about how his muscles look, and not try to overpower his training partner, his movements take on a greater fluidity. He will begin to understand and enjoy how the mechanics of the move, along with his energy, makes the suspect grimace. Once he has achieved that, he can then bring that hard-earned exterior muscle along for the ride, a ride the suspect will hate.

I don't want to spend time and space in this book illustrating weight lifting and cardio exercise. The interested reader wanting to know in detail about training and nutrition will find tons of information in *The Fighter's Body: An Owner's Manual: Your Guide to Diet, Nutrition, Exercise and Excellence in the Martial Arts* by Wim Demeere and me, also available through Turtle Press. However, I do want to comment briefly on why you should lift and why you should train for cardio fitness.

Weight Training

Here is a revelation that will sit you back on your heels: weight training makes you stronger. As obvious as this would seem, why doesn't every law enforcement officer lift? Being stronger makes hauling that injured person down the stairs easier and that drunk up the stairs. It helps you push that car out of the intersection easier and, for you county deputies, it helps you get that tipped cow back up on its hooves.

You can do all those things now, you say. True, but when you're strong, you do them easier and with less chance of injury. Strength gives you confidence and looking strong makes some people think twice about resisting.

Fast-twitch muscle fibers

When you push the heavy weights, a poundage that makes your neck cords stick out on the final 8th rep, you not only gain strength but you stimulate your fast-twitch muscle fibers. While you can't increase the number of these fibers, you can make them stronger, which in turn makes you faster. Don't wait until some vermin is pointing a gun at you within your reach, to think, "Gee, I wish I were faster."

Greater speed provides you with a better chance to:

- grab or deflect that threatening weapon.

- block that incoming punch, push or kick.

- apply a control hold before the suspect can resist.

- leap out of the way of that car sliding toward you.

- grab that bridge jumper.

- duck the sergeant when he's looking for someone for a crappy detail.

If the idea of lifting weights makes you want to lie in a hammock under a tree, know that you only have to do three or four sets of five exercises, which takes about 20 minutes. Wearing those tiny posing trunks is optional.

Here is what you should do, and why:

Bench presses

Use a barbell or dumbbells. With dumbbells, more muscles are involved to keep them balanced. Do 3 or 4 sets of 8 heavy reps.

Benches work your chest, shoulders, upper back, neck and arms, which increase your strength and speed to:

- Push a person away, push a door open, push a vehicle out of the street.

- Punch or palm-heel strike a suspect.

- Get you up from the ground quickly.

- Hold someone down on the ground.

Barbell or dumbbell rowing or lat machine pull downs

Do 3 or 4 sets of 8 heavy reps. These work your back, arms and core, which increase your speed and strength to:

- Pull a person, pull a door, pull other objects

- Lift a suspect or object up from the ground

- Pull yourself over a fence

Triceps

Your triceps get worked hard doing the benches (which you should do first), so you need only 2 or 3 sets, 6 to 8 reps of your favorite rear-arm exercise: weighted dips, close-grip bench press, lat-machine press downs, and so on. You benefit in speed and strength the same as you do with benches.

Biceps

You worked your biceps when you did the rowing or pull downs (which you should do first) so you need only 2 or 3 sets of 6 to 8 reps. Barbell curls and dumbbell curls still reign supreme. You benefit in speed and strength the same as you do with rowing and pull downs.

Squats

The nice side benefit of doing squats – besides looking awesome at the police picnic in your cutoff jeans – is that working them stimulates a small degree of growth in all your muscles. Your primary objective with squats is to develop a powerful base. Skip the leg extension machine because it can be hard on your knees. Use a squat machine, a barbell squat rack or simply grab a couple of dumbbells, and hold them down at your sides. Do 3 sets of 8 to 10 hard reps. You benefit in stability, speed and strength to:

- resist a push or hard charge.

- push something or someone.

- pull something or someone.

- kick something or someone.

- pick up something or someone.

- force a resisting suspect to walk.

Aerobic and anaerobic

An aerobic exercise, which translates to "with oxygen," is any activity that uses large muscles, is somewhat rhythmic, and is continuous. It pushes the heart and lungs to work hard – around 70 to 80 percent of maximum heart rate. Jogging for a mile is aerobic, as is swimming laps and popping out medium intensity punches and kicks for 20 minutes.

An anaerobic exercise translates to "without air" or sometimes "without oxygen." This is different from aerobic. Anaerobic activity is done at high intensity and requires a rate of energy production greater than that supplied by aerobic respiration. An anaerobic state kicks in fast when you're engaged in a desperate, all-out fight with a suspect. If you lack such conditioning, you suddenly feel weak, you're sucking for air like a beached carp, and you're hoping you can last.

During my martial arts competitive years, I worked a beat in Portland's skid row, a true Wild West show around the clock. While I was in good shape aerobically and could easily do an hour of moderate sparring, I couldn't understand why I would cough and wheeze after a minute of thrashing around full-bore with a combative suspect. Later I learned it was because I hadn't trained anaerobically, which is to say I hadn't prepared for the realities of a hard street fight. Cops need both aerobic and anaerobic exercises.

Here are some things to consider when putting a fitness program together:

- An aerobics only program – jogging, tennis, Stairmaster, treadmill – strengthens your heart and lungs, but fails to develop upper body strength or anaerobic fitness.

- Weight training only – benches, curls, squats - develops physical strength but not aerobic and anaerobic fitness.

- Anaerobic training only – sprinting, hard bag punching and kicking – helps you survive a sudden, explosive encounter, but doesn't give you the endurance needed for working a double shift on a walking beat, running for several minutes, or the muscular strength to overcome great resistance.

Clearly, you need a program that includes strength, as well as aerobic and anaerobic conditioning. The good news is that it's easy to do.

- Put together a 20-minute weight training program that works the areas mentioned earlier. Lift no more than twice a week.

- Do an aerobic exercise for 20 to 30 minutes. You can save time and combine aerobic training with weight training: lift weights using a circuit system where you proceed nonstop through the exercises three or four times:

  o 1 set of benches

  o 1 set of pull downs

  o 1 set of curls

  o 1 set of dips

  o 1 set of squats.

Rest for 30 seconds and do it again. You won't be able to lift as much at first as when you rested between sets, but that's okay because your muscles don't know the difference. The weight feels heavy no matter what the poundage reads.

- Once a week do an anaerobic exercise for 20 minutes. For example:

  o Jog for 90 seconds and then sprint all out for 30 seconds. Repeat until your session is over.

  o Work the heavy bag, punching, kicking and/or striking it with your baton. Hit for 90 seconds at a comfortable aerobic pace and then go all-out for 30 seconds. Repeat until your session is over.

I've got two posters in my training area. One shows a man in a martial arts uniform, a hard-looking dude with a face that looks like he could eat a kitten. The text on the poster lists all the crimes he's done and how much he hates the cops. The last sentence notes that he just earned his 5th-degree black belt.

The other poster shows a prison con, a giant of a man, squatting with a huge barbell, the weights on each end equivalent to two Toyota Corollas. The text asks if you have missed many workouts lately... and then notes that the man in the photo hasn't.

If these aren't an incentive to train...

Joint Manipulation and Leverage Control

Officers who don't like joint locks say:

- they are mostly ineffective.

- they only work on the training mat.

- they don't work when the suspect resists intensely.

- they rely too much on fine motor control.

- you have to be too close to the suspect.

While there are shades of truth to these under certain circumstances, there are solutions. Here are my quick responses; we examine the issues as we proceed.

• Joint locks are mostly ineffective

Aikido is a martial art that is mildly controversial among other fighters who practice what they deem to be more hardcore fighting systems. When someone proclaimed to the salty old aikido master that his art was ineffective, the old one responded, "Aikido is effective; but yours isn't." Police joint locks and leverage control holds are highly effective, but they require practice and intelligent application, i.e., a good understanding of how, when, why and where to use them. I recall an Arkansas trooper telling me in his slow drawl, "Yuh wouldn't do one of them thar fancy wrist locks on a big ol' country boy comin' at yuh with a whirlin' chain saw." This is true. Wisdom helps your success rate.

• They only work on the training mat

Most often, techniques work better on the mat because conditions are more sanitary, controlled, and there is more cooperation from your training partner than what you get on the street. Sometimes this is just the way it is because the agency, concerned about injury, forbids all-out resistance. I once allowed a recruit class to practice without restraint. Two days later, I had to stop after the DA's office complained about clocks and diplomas falling when students in the adjoining training room smashed into the wall we shared. Additionally, a student suffered permanent facial scarring, another suffered a severe knee injury from a baton strike, and an ambulance carried off another recruit. Today there are full-body padding, partial body padding, soft batons, and other protective equipment that allows hardcore training to be more effective and safe. Check police and martial arts equipment outlets to see what all is available.

• They don't work when the suspect is resisting intensely

Yes they do, but you must know how and when to apply them. When the environment isn't conducive to drawing your weapon, and moving in for a joint lock isn't wise, you need to "soften" the suspect first with a kick, a chair across his head or, as I did once, drape him with a mattress. Then you apply a control hold. Or, when your hold starts out fine but you meet great resistance half way into it, you either have to switch to a leverage move or soften him with a blow.

• They rely too much on fine motor control

Actually, the beauty of these moves is that they don't. They are no more fine motor than drawing your weapon or pulling your baton. In fact, they require less fine motor skill than performing functions on your car computer or radio.

• You have to be close to the suspect

Well, you got me there. Probably what this officer meant was that you have to move across the gap between you and the suspect. Doing so is indeed dangerous but it's all about timing, positioning and distraction. We cover these issues as we look at the techniques that follow.

Finger Techniques

Definition: Yubi tori are the Japanese words for finger techniques, sometimes shortened to yubies (you-bees) by jujitsu people. Yubies occur anytime you twist, stretch, crumple or bend a finger or fingers in a way they weren't designed to move.

Finger techniques are subtle, excruciatingly painful and most importantly, they work more times than not. As a skid row beat cop who wrestled with the extremely inebriated on a daily basis, finger techniques were my bread-and-butter moves, the pain from which nearly always penetrated brains pickled from years of alcohol abuse. In addition, as a member of one of the many arrest teams sent into action whenever there was a violent protest, I used finger techniques to get people off the ground, move them through hordes of TV cameras, and out of the midst of their compatriots. This was all done while appearing as if I weren't remotely responsible for the person yelping and carrying on.

War story

Curtis Sliwa, founder of the Guardian Angels, came to town once to join in with dozens of other protestors who were upset about something involving the homeless. Several of them chained themselves to the doors of a building (if I'd been chief for a day, I'd have ordered all the officers to resume normal patrol and let them sit on the cold asphalt with their arms chained to door handles).

When Sliwa showed up, there weren't any door handles left so he just sat on the sidewalk. Television cameras zoomed in as I bent down to tell him that he was under arrest. He said he understood but that he wasn't moving. Again, I told him to get up and he said he wouldn't because he was protesting. I bent farther and said into his ear that I would use force and he whispered back for me to do what I had to do.

Sliwa looked to be a solid 200 pounds and I wasn't about to strain my gizzard lifting him in view of the salivating cameras. So, I slapped on the handcuffs and grasped his upper arm. When I felt his body tense to make himself heavy, I grabbed his little finger and ring finger with my other hand and flexed them back a couple inches beyond where they normally go.

Mr. Sliwa got up so quickly that I had to step back so that he didn't knock me over. The 5 o'clock news showed him standing up in a hurry but the cameras didn't detect the technique that made him do so.

LOW VISIBILITY

Bending or twisting a digit is a low profile move that draws little attention to what you're doing and can save you extra problems when moving a biker out of a crowded biker bar, a violent protestor away from his peers, or a drunken movie patron up the aisle of a packed theater. Onlookers haven't a clue what you're doing, though they wonder why the person you're arresting isn't balking. Of course, there are the occasional recipients of finger techniques who scream bloody murder, "Yooowww! You're breaking my finger!" That blows your cover and ruins everything.

Elements of Applying Finger Techniques

Finger techniques are simple. You know the mobility range of your fingers and at what point pushing them beyond that hurts. That range is similar – give or take a couple inches - to that of every other humanoid. If it hurts you, it's likely to hurt the drunken husband you need to move out of the house.

Here are the classic moves:

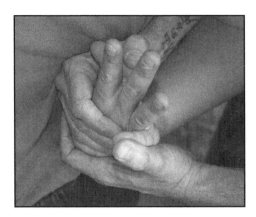

Across

Push his little finger across his other fingers

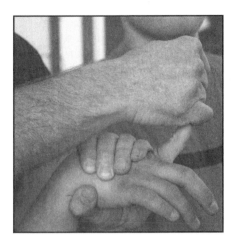

Bend

Grasp a finger and bend it back.

Compressing

Compress a bent finger in your palm

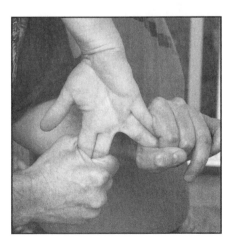

Split

Pull two fingers in opposite directions.

Warning: Be cautious about slamming on the force as finger bones are easily broken and their tendons and ligaments easily damaged. Now, if you're in a desperate struggle for your life, grab the suspect's fingers and attack them with all the juice you have. However, in situations in which you're striving to control the suspect, it's safest to apply pressure slowly to split, compress, and bend until you get the desired result. Good training will help understand how far you can push a finger into the red pain zone.

Applications

Across

This small and subtle movement doesn't look like much, but it just might be the deciding factor whether you establish, maintain or lose control of the suspect. Lift the finger up as far as it can go and push it across the next closest finger. If he's flexible, push it across the next finger after that.

Wrist flex helper

Hook the thumb around his little finger and push it across his ring finger.

Your hold is hurting the suspect but not enough to elicit his cooperation.

Handcuff position

You have locked the suspect's hand behind him but he seems to be tolerating much of the pain.

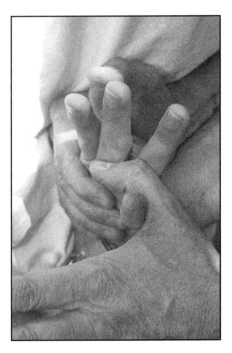

Maintain the flex with your inside hand and hook his little finger with your other.

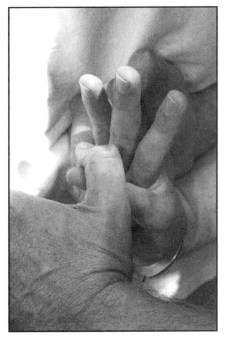

Jam it across his ring finger until he complies with your commands.

Against a wall brace

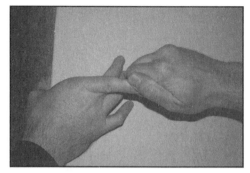

Immediately, hook a finger and push it across his others.

You're moving the suspect from point A to point B when he braces a hand on the wall.

When he pulls his hand away, push him through the door or move his arm to a control position.

Bend

Just because a person is handcuffed doesn't mean he won't act stupid and make you look foolish as you struggle with him. However, when you latch onto a finger of a cuffed hand and give it a little crank, most arrestees will see things your way.

Against a handcuffed suspect

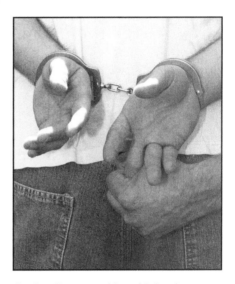

Grab a finger and bend it back.

You caught and cuffed him. Now you want to move him but he's balking.

As you bend his finger, use your other hand to push or pull him in the direction you want him to go. Give him verbal commands, too.

Against a seated suspect

I used this often against seated drunks who refused to get up. Instead of injuring my back lifting them, I'd bend a finger, the pinpoint pain of which penetrated the pickled brain, encouraging the person to get up on their own.

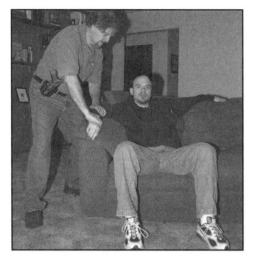

A drunk (or an obnoxious sober person) refuses to get up.

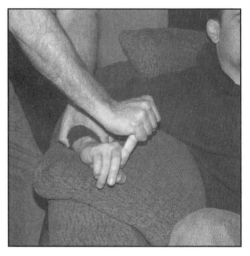

Grab his finger and bend it back.

Rotate your hand a little – a nearly imperceptible movement – forcing his heel forward in the direction you want him to move.

Slap on a wristlock when he gets up.

Against a grip on a steering wheel

The suspect grips the steering wheel and refuses to get out.

To divide his attention, gouge the hollow behind his ear as you simultaneously pull at his stiffened finger.

Grab his wrist and commence to armbar him out of the car.

AN ADDITIONAL TOOL

You might look at the scenario examples here and wonder why you would use a finger technique when there are armbars, leg sweeps and other "bigger" alternatives. However, another officer will look at other scenarios in this book and think that a finger technique would have worked just fine as opposed to, say, the armlock that was shown.

It all boils down to what you're comfortable with given your skill level and what you deem the best technique given the existing elements in a situation. If you can gain control or escape from a grab with a subtle, low-keyed finger tweak, that is arguably better than a larger motion, such as a shoulder lock takedown. This is especially true in an environment populated by the suspect's friends or where there is a reporter wanting to make a cop look bad.

At the most, you just might become a master of finger warfare. At the least, you have one more tool in your little red toolbox.

Compressing

This is a little harder to get than the other yubies but worth the effort to master.

Against a wrist grab

A subject shakes your hand but then won't release it.

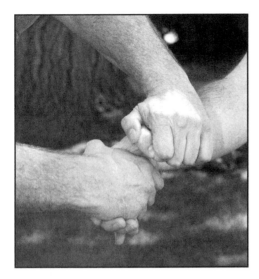

Grab his thumb so that you're pressing the tip against your index finger. Then push against the back of his thumb with your thumb and squeeze.

Most people will release their grip. (You know you're doing it correctly when your training partner tells you that it feels as if his thumb were being crushed.)

When handcuffed

This is a good come-a-long hold when your handcuffed suspect balks.

You're walking the suspect when he abruptly refuses to move.

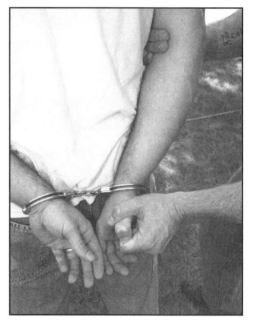

Secure his arm. With your other hand, grab his thumb so that the tip presses into your index finger and your thumb presses against its base. Now squeeze.

Expect him to yelp in pain. When he starts walking again, slack off on the pain but maintain the grip. Keep hold of his upper arm.

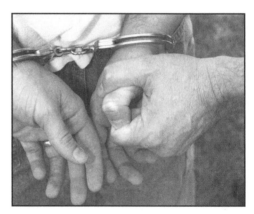

Splits

I remember seeing a movie where gladiators tied one end of a rope around a captor's right ankle and the other end around a horse facing north. They did the same thing to his other ankle and tied the other end to a horse facing south. Then the gladiators slapped the horses' rumps, forcing the hapless prisoner into a serious case of the splits. (Let's pause for a moment to envision that scene) That's sort of what happens with this technique except there are no horses, no rope, and no ankles involved.

Bent arm wrist twist

You're applying a wrist twist when the suspect begins to defeat it.

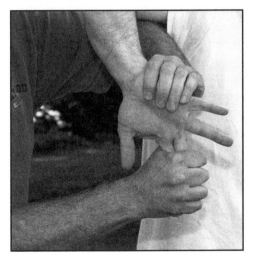

Drop your outside hand to grasp his little finger and ring finger...

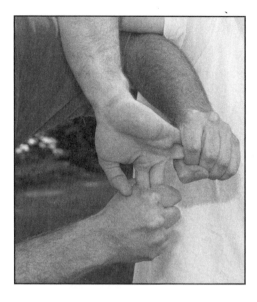

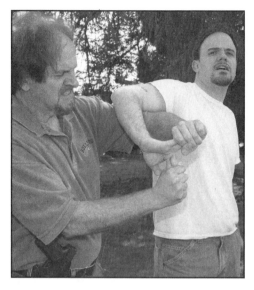

...and your inside hand to his index and middle finger.

Let him see you pulling his fingers apart as you command him to stop resisting. The command and the visual are powerful bedfellows.

Against a face push

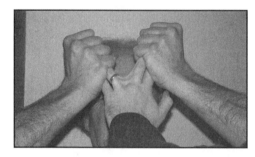

Grab his fingers and pull them apart as you jerk his hand downward. Proceed with a takedown of your choice.

The suspect pushes you against a wall with his hand on your face.

Note: You can grab any number of fingers with each hand: two fingers in each, one finger in one and two or three in the other.

The Versatile Wristlock

Most police agencies under-use the wristlock, limiting it to a come-a-long hold or a setup position to handcuffing. This is unfortunate because there are so many other situations in which to use it and variations as to how it's done.

War story

One time I arrested an outlaw biker, flexcuffed him and was pressing him against a wall yelling at him to stop resisting as I applied ever-increasing pressure on a wristlock. Just as I was thinking that he might be impervious to the pain, I heard a loud pop, not as loud as a .22 round, but close, and I felt the tension in his wrist give way. For the first time since I'd been cranking on the hold, I saw his face change expression, not much, just a little grimace. Realizing that his muscular wrist had just broken like a thick tree branch, I let it go, scooted around to his other side and applied a wristlock on that hand.

He was cooperative after that.

I learned later that this particular bike club followed a code of not showing pain, especially to the police. I wish now that I would have asked him, "So, how's that code workin' for yuh?" as they encased his hand in a cast.

Elements of the Wristlock

By wrapping one or two hands around the back of the suspect's hand and pressing it toward his braced elbow, his wrist tendons stretch painfully farther than they do normally.

Here are a few important elements about this classic hold:

- Without the elbow brace, the technique won't work to affect pain.

- As mentioned, this simple configuration works in a variety of positions, which we examine in this chapter.

- Stretching the innards of the wrist doesn't hurt everyone, though it hurts most.

- You can increase the pain without significantly changing the position.

- It's rare, but there are people who possess such extreme flexibility that their palm can lie flat on the underside of their forearm. This technique won't work on them.

- Some people possess wrists so stiff that even the slightest pressure on their hand causes them great pain. Don't think they are faking or resisting.

- Some eat the pain and continue to resist no matter how intense. We don't like these people.

- Use the wristlock to hold a suspect in place, to force him to the floor, to force him to stand up, and to force him to move left, right, forward and back.

Standing Suspect

Let's look at a few ways to use the wristlock to make a suspect stand fast.

Basic entry: From minimum custody

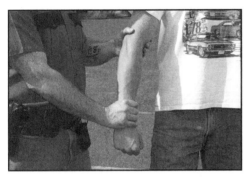

You're holding the suspect by his wrist and elbow.

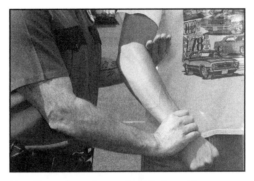

Use the edge of your inside hand to press into the front of his elbow. Don't insert your wrist because it's easy for the suspect to tighten his arm and trap you.

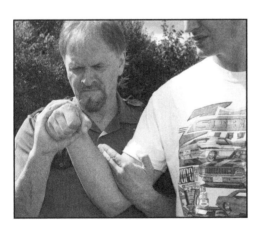

As you bend the inside of his elbow, push his wrist toward his shoulder.

As his forearm nears vertical, slide your hand down to the back of his hand and begin to move your inside hand...

...up to join it.

Don't let your hands extend onto his fingers. They bend so flexing them won't hurt.

Don't grip his wrist as it doesn't bend; only the joint does. Stay on the back of his hand.

Don't fail to wrap your thumbs underneath because he can easily escape by snapping his wrist downward.

Do wrap one or both thumbs underneath.

Bury his elbow into your abdomen or against your chest.

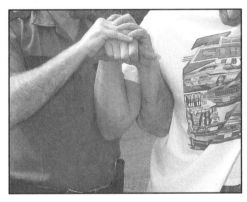

Sometimes you might need to place his elbow into the crook of your arm. That's okay, but you need to remain mindful as it isn't as solid as the other two places.

Command him to spread his feet, to slow his mobility, and to place his free hand on top of his head, so you know where it is at all times.

Entry from the front

The steps are similar whether you're approaching from the front, side or back.

Reach out to grab his wrist.

Pull the inside of his elbow to begin bending his arm.

Step forward and turn into him, bumping his shoulder to distract him for a hair of a second as you simultaneously...

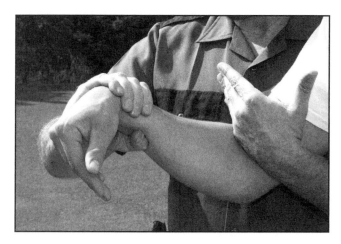

...pop his elbow and lift his wrist.

Slide your closest hand down onto his hand and then your inside hand.

Entry from a push

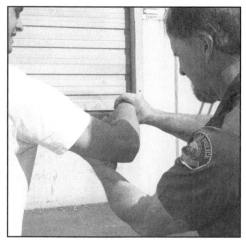

You block the suspect's push. (left)

Grab his wrist with your other hand as you move into him. (above)

Simultaneously bump him, press his elbow and push his hand toward his shoulder. (left)

Conclude with both of your hands cranking his. (above)

Applying the wristlock behind the suspect

While this lock and position is a common handcuffing position, it's also an effective tool to move a suspect a short distance. For example, when you don't want to handcuff a thug in a tavern with his buddies all around you, use this to quickly escort him out the door and over to your car. Then without changing position, slap on the restraints.

Entry from the front:

Step so that you're perpendicular to him as you move his hand behind his back.

You decide to take the suspect into custody. Close the distance as you simultaneously reach for his right elbow and hand. Note that your right palm is facing upward as your thumb points toward the suspect.

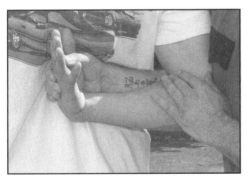

Notice that your right arm is next to his back, not over his arm or under it.

Command him, as you flex his wrist, to place his other hand on his head. If you choose not to handcuff right away, walk him backwards as you apply pain.

Entry from a bent-arm wristlock:

Note: While it takes a few seconds to read the step-by-step instruction, when done smoothly, it should take about five seconds.

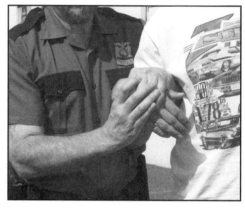

Simultaneously turn his fingers toward his body without reducing the pressure in his wrist, and release your outside hand.

You have applied the wristlock to control him while you ask questions, or to move him a short distance. Now you want to cuff him.

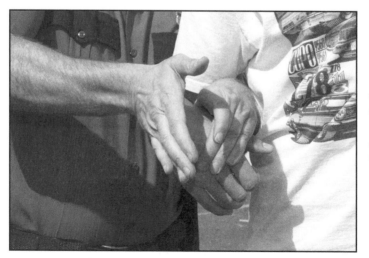

Lower his flexed hand until his forearm is about horizontal with the ground. His fingers touch his side. Place the edge of your outside hand onto his wrist...

... and replace your inside hand with your outside. Your inside hand grips his upper arm to control it and to assist moving his arm behind his back.

Turn your body so that it's perpendicular to the suspect as you push his hand and arm across his lower back. Release his upper arm so that hand can assist your other. Command him to put his free hand on top of his head.

SMOOTHNESS OVER SPEED

Strive for smooth handcuffing rather than trying to race the clock. Speed tends to create errors so that critical steps deteriorate. When officers try to be super fast:

- they lose control of the suspect's wrist.

- they drop their cuffs.

- they cuff their own hands.

- they lose prisoners.

Train for smoothness of technique, not speed. When you can talk to someone about going fishing as you execute the technique, and do so smoothly, you have arrived. Training this way creates error-free execution that will eventually be fast, at least as fast as most situations require.

Downed Suspect

Use the wristlock to hold a prone suspect immobile or to supplement other locks.

On his stomach - Arm extended

You have taken the suspect down with an armbar.

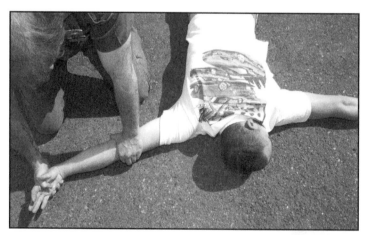

Push his arm upward so that it's at a 45-degree angle (which prevents him from rolling toward you) and wrap your hand around the back of his hand. Press inward as you press your weight onto his elbow. Your weight on his elbow creates a base. A partner would apply the wristlock the same way on his other arm

On his stomach - Arm upright:

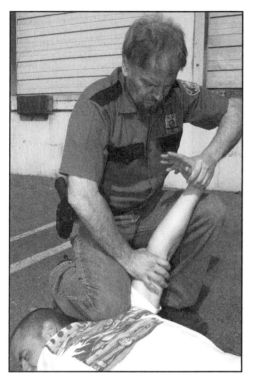

You have elevated his arm and you're pressing down on the back of his hand. Elevate your elbow as shown to maximize your power.

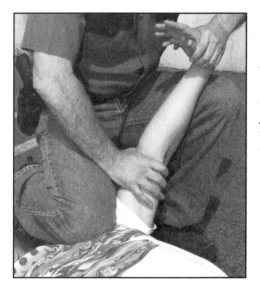

There are actually four ways to affect pain in this position: 1) push down on the back of his hand; 2) apply pressure on his elbow joint; 3) push his arm toward his head to stretch his shoulder socket; 4) push down on his arm to jam his shoulder joint.

On his stomach - Arm bent prone:

You have moved his arm behind his back.

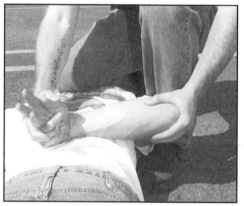

Insert your foot under his ribs so that your shinbone blocks the back of his arm. Without this brace, the technique is useless. I used to flunk recruits for not doing it. You can flex his hand using this grip or...

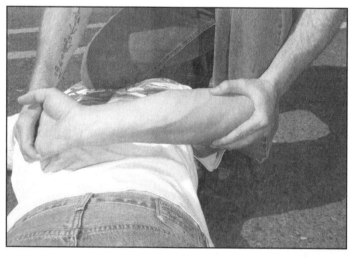

...this reverse grip, in which you bend his fingers back and push his heel outward.

On his stomach - Arm bent supine:

I don't advise doing this technique by yourself since the suspect can easily roll toward you. It works great, though, when your partner has a hold of some kind on his other arm. Also, there isn't a smooth way to handcuff from this position. The few times I've used it alone were those occasions when I didn't want to risk turning over a violent suspect. So I used this excruciatingly painful hold for a few seconds to convince the guy to stop resisting before I proceeded to roll him for cuffing.

Warning 1: It takes very little pressure to affect pain and just a little more to affect injury.

Warning 2: Whenever you transition a suspect from one position to another, such as rolling him from his back onto his stomach, there is a weakness, a moment in time for him to resist or escape. Yes, you can administer pain through your transition technique, but few are as strong as when the suspect is motionless. Your best option is to wait for backup. If there isn't help coming, transition only when your gut tells you it's okay to do so.

Arm bent supine - Using the floor as a base:

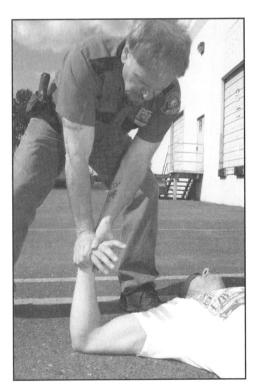

The suspect's arm is bent 90 degrees. Using the floor as the base, press down on the back of his hand.

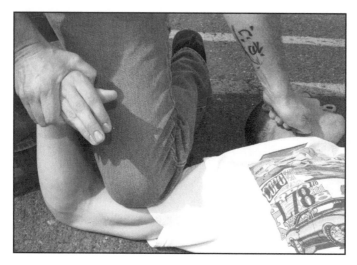

To add more pain, place your knee on his tender biceps. Use your other hand to push his head away from you by digging your middle knuckles under his jaw line. Most people will move their head away, which distracts them from resisting.

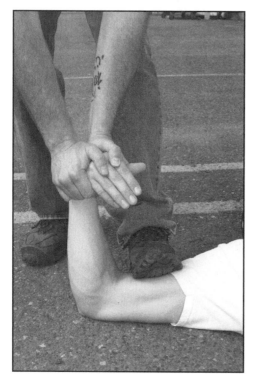

Grinding your foot into his biceps works well, but it's doesn't look good PR wise.

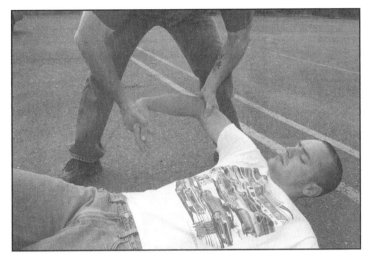

To roll him over: Scoop your hand under his elbow to maintain a base and lift his arm so that it's parallel with his upper body. Squeeze his elbow toward the flexed wrist...

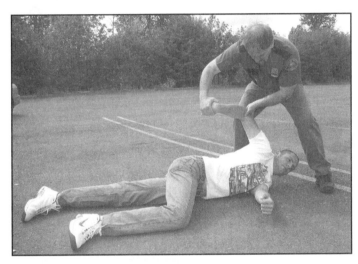

...walk around his head (never step over his body) ...

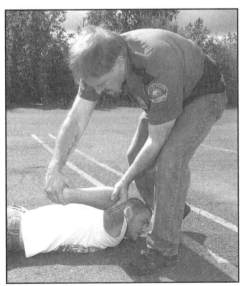

...and watch him flip over like a beached fish.

Arm bent supine - Using your body as base:

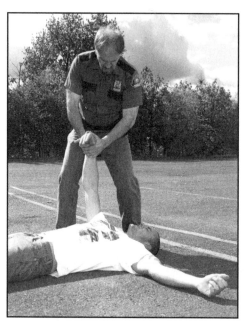

You have dumped the suspect onto his back. Hold onto his wrist.

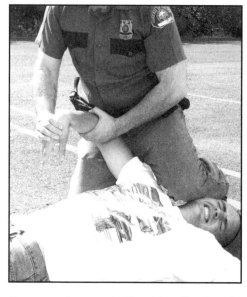

Press one knee onto the side of his head and lower the other to the ground. Press his elbow to fold his arm.

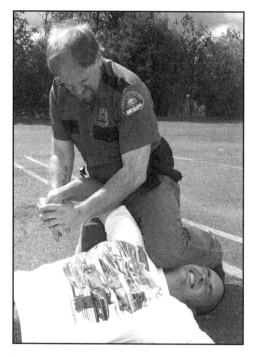

Pull the back of his hand toward his braced elbow.

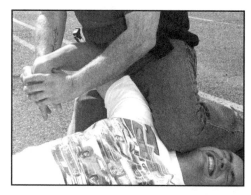

Hold him in this position until you get help or follow the rollover procedure as shown in "Using the floor as a base" technique.

On his side

You have taken him down and he has landed on his side. Keep hold of his arm.

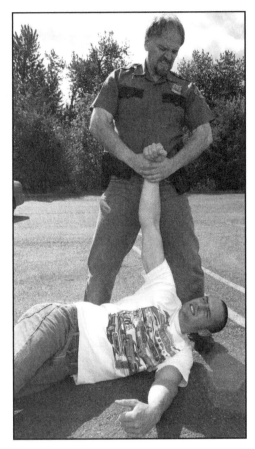

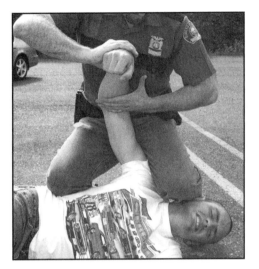

Simultaneously, lower one knee onto his head and one into his ribs. This pins him to the ground and helps provide a base. The instant your knees land, press his elbow with your hand closest to his head to fold his forearm downward.

Lift him by his wrist to take the play out of his arm and to wedge him snuggly onto his side. He can't kick or punch you from this position.

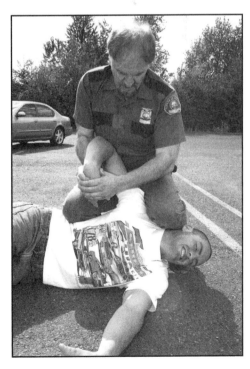

Slide the hand gripping his wrist over the back of his hand and cover that hand with your other. Brace his elbow against your abdomen as you pull the back of his hand to stretch his wrist tendons. Hold him in this position until you get help or follow the rollover procedure as shown in "Using the floor as a base" technique.

Wristlock takedowns

These takedown techniques work amazingly well because they employ a combination of pain and leverage. Use them to dump someone onto their rear and then use the above rollover techniques to get them onto their stomach for cuffing. They also work well when you insist that your cranky suspect have a seat in the interview room.

From the standing wristlock: straight down

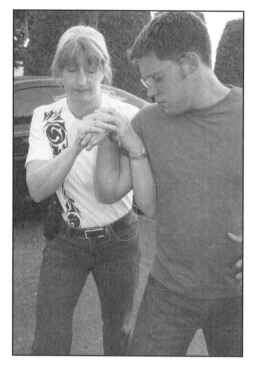

You're restraining the suspect with a standard lock. To take him to the ground...

...maintain the lock with your outside hand and remove your inside one. [To show the technique, Lisa is standing farther away from the suspect than normal.]

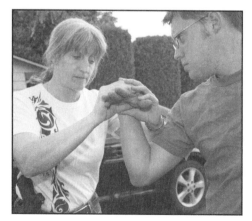

Place your inside hand back onto his hand but outside his arm (this eliminates his elbow base) and simultaneously...

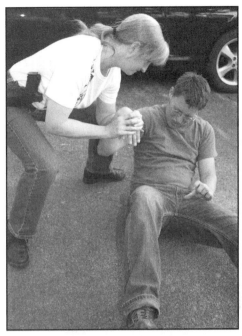

...move your inside foot back a little so that you're standing perpendicular to him. Apply pressure on the back of his hand, using your forearms to keep his arm straight, and crouch as he begins to drop. He drops because there is no base.

Follow him to the ground, but stay on your feet, and maintain control of his wrist.

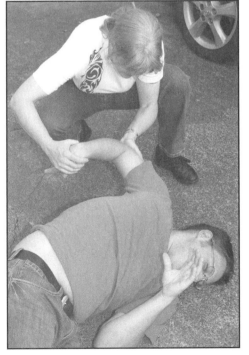

To roll him over, maintain the flex with your outside hand and create a base on his elbow with your other.

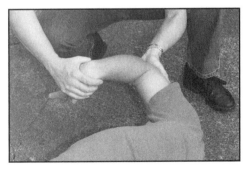

Follow the rollover procedure as shown in "Using the floor as a base" technique.

Takedown into a chair

You're restraining the suspect with the same wristlock and you want him to sit.

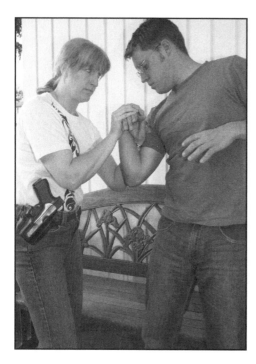

Simultaneously, maintain the lock with your outside hand, move your inside hand out from between his arm and side, and place it on top of his hand.

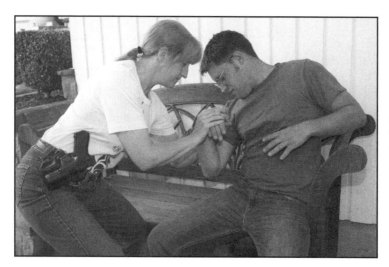

Press down on the back of his hand, ensuring that his forearm remains vertical, until he plops into the seat.

Takedown over backwards

He's getting too physical so you decide to take him down onto his back.

From the control position...

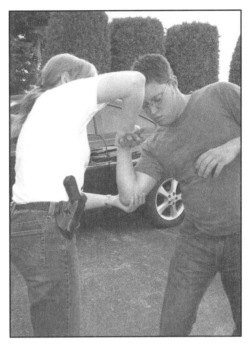

...stay in close to him [Lisa is standing slightly away to show the technique] to maximize your strength. If you step too far away, you lose strength and control, and he might escape.

Squeeze the back of his hand and his elbow toward each other as...

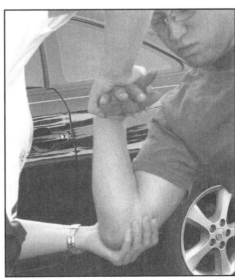

...you tilt his arm back. Do this by pulling his elbow forward slightly and pushing his hand back slightly.

Note: You lose some stability in your hold at this point so you must execute the move smoothly and quickly. His body follows the direction of his wrist. To keep up with him, you have to take a step or two in the direction he's falling.

Free tip: Don't think "I'm pushing his body down" but rather "I'm driving his wrist back and down." Think of it that way and his body just has to come along for the ride.

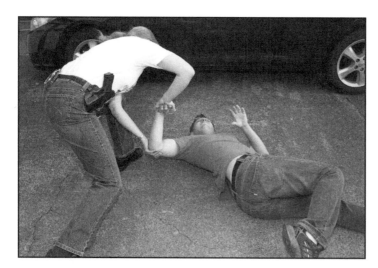

He lands. Keep compressing his wrist and elbow to flip him onto his stomach.

Take him down in a circle

This is a good Plan B should the suspect step back to try to negate your "straight back and down" takedown. The circle weakens his balance. The first part of this technique is the same as the last one so let's start with the takedown.

You have the suspect in the wristlock control hold when he steps back to resist. Quickly move your inside hand down to his elbow and compress the back of his hand toward it as you tilt his arm back about 45 degrees.

Keep compressing as you step outward to your left with your left foot. Don't pull on his arm as you might lose the position. Just tilt and compress as you step.

Continue to turn him in a circle until he goes down.

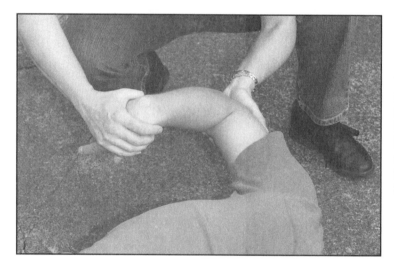

Turn his arm so that his hand is toward his legs and his elbow toward his head and then compress the two to flip him onto his stomach.

So why not always take him in a circle? You can. It's just a matter of preference.

When the suspect resists your grab

You're pulling the suspect's arm (not a sound tactic) ...

...and he resists by pulling his arm, and you, back.

Step toward his pull and slide your right hand onto the back of his hand as you move your left to cup his elbow. Tilt his arm back...

...and proceed to take him down. To turn him over, turn his arm so that his hand is toward his legs and his elbow toward his head as you did in the last sequence.

Wristlock Pickups

I used these all the time when I worked skidrow and as a member of an arrest team during demonstrations. You need to be careful because when you pick up someone by their wrist, much of their body weight shifts to that joint. Be sure to use verbal commands so that he knows what you want him to do.

Sitting cross legged

This is a favorite passive resistance position used by protestors. First, you have to get their arm.

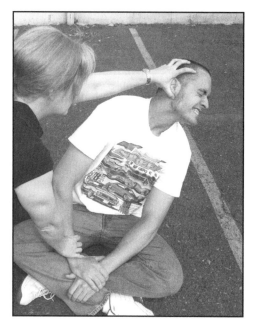

Should the protestor resist giving you his arm, push your thumb into his mastoid or any other nerve point of your choice.

Jerk his arm free, cup his elbow...

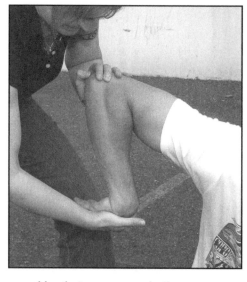

... and begin to compress both.

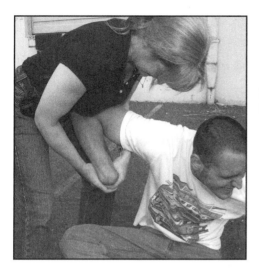

Variation: Use your abdomen or chest to brace his elbow.

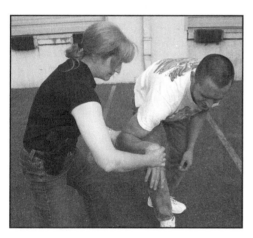

When he is about half way up, rotate his forearm...

...until its turned over. Brace his elbow against your body and use both of your hands to apply pressure to his wrist.

Sitting on stairs

Follow the same procedure as just shown in "Sitting cross legged."

Secure his wrist and elbow.

Force his arm into a vertical, and squeeze his hand and elbow toward each other.

Roll his arm over when he is half way up, jam his elbow into your chest or abdomen and move him away from the stairs. Note: Because of the height difference in this case, Lisa holds the suspect's arm at a slight angle rather than vertical. That's okay, but you need to be especially cognizant that he doesn't slip out of the hold.

From the prone

Sometimes you get a suspect who refuses to get up. Don't blow a disc; use the wristlock.

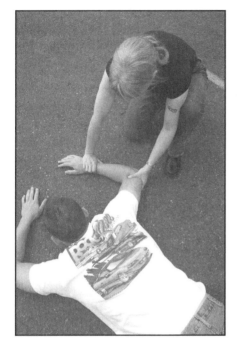

Grab his wrist and the inside of his elbow.

Position his arm vertically and compress his hand and elbow.

Continue to squeeze as he gets up, even harder if he balks along the way. Note: Since it isn't easy getting up when someone is holding one of your support hands, don't get too cranky if he doesn't stand as quickly as you think he should. Know the difference between the effort it takes to get up and someone refusing to get up.

About half way up, rotate his arm until his forearm is close to vertical. Brace his elbow against your body and use both of your hands to apply pressure.

From the supine

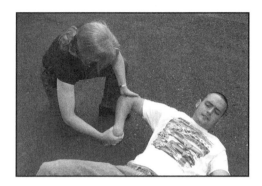

Secure his hand and elbow.

Move it into a bent arm position and, as you apply pressure to his wrist, use verbal commands to order him to stand.

When he is half way up, begin to roll his arm over.

Brace his elbow against your body and use both hands to apply pressure.

Baseless upward jam

This technique doesn't cause great pain because there is no base, but it does give direction for a brief moment. So, before he gyrates out of it, grab his arm and flow into any of the other techniques shown in this text. In the scenario shown here, you can keep pushing him so that he stumbles on the steps or simply yank his arm toward you to pull him off the stairs.

A suspect on a stairwell reaches down for you.

Grab his hand with both of yours, your heels pressing on the back of his.

Flex it upward with a snapping motion.

Wrist Twist and Inverted Flex

This is a bread-n-butter technique of mine, one I've used many times. It doesn't rely on strength and it doesn't matter how strong the suspect is. All you need is the opportunity to apply it. There are two versions: the wrist twist and the inverted flex.

Elements of the Wrist Twist

Reach straight across, grasp his hand with your thumb, and press the back of his hand between his pointy finger and middle finger. Your other fingers wrap around the base of his thumb.

Swing his hand up about as high as his face. Press the thumb of your other hand into the back of his hand between his little and middle fingers. Your other fingers wrap around the edge of his palm.

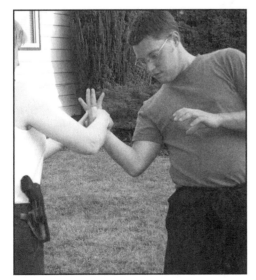

His forearm and upper arm are bent about 45 degrees as you twist his hand outward. When it locks, the suspect's body shifts in that same direction. Turn your foot closest to the direction he is leaning...

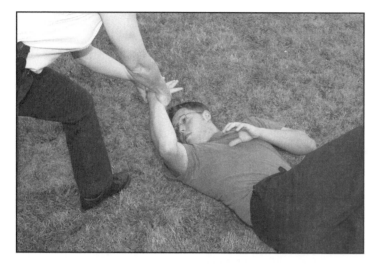

...to take him down.

Occasionally, a suspect leans with the twist but won't fall. Maybe his wrist doesn't lock or you've erred in the application. To fix the problem, simply push his head down.

Don't step across with your other foot. This common error is unnecessary and places you off balance.

Applications

Push

Do all four steps in one continuous motion.

This might be a push or a shirt grab. Rotate your body away from his arm as you grip his hand as described above.

Rotate your body back as your other hand grasps his hand.

Continue to turn toward the outside of his arm as you twist his hand outward.

Down he goes.

Wrist or arm grab

It doesn't matter which of your arms he grabs or which of his he grabs with. The instant he encircles your wrist or arm, rotate your palm upward as you lift your arm up and toward the direction of his grabbing arm. This action positions his hand for you to twist.

He grabs your right wrist.

Swing your arm up and reach toward the back of his hand with your free hand.

Jerk your trapped hand free in the direction his gripping thumb points. Some teachers say to pull toward the opening between the thumb and fingers. I think it's more effective to pull toward the tip of the thumb.

...Latch on with your now free hand and take him down as before.

Pain compliance in the supine

This is painful option when you can't or don't want to roll the suspect over. You can't hold him here for long, but it's really hurts until you decide your next move.

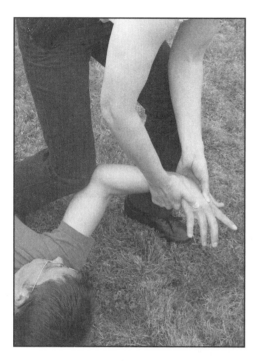

He lands. Place your closest knee into the small indention about two inches from his elbow and continue to twist his hand outward. This hurts because when you twist his hand, his elbow moves in the opposite direction an inch or two. But when your knee prevents his elbow from moving, all of the energy (pain) goes into the joint.

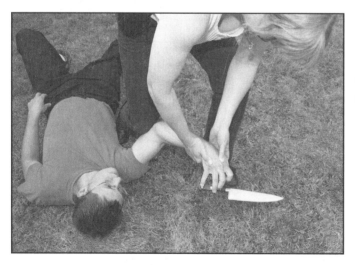

This works to force him to release a weapon, too.

Roll over into the prone

This is a classic rollover into the prone that works well with the wrist twist. You will see it again with other techniques.

Jerk his arm up the moment he lands so he can't hit you with his feet or hands.

Apply pressure against his elbow in the direction you want him to roll, and walk around his head.

Keep walking and pressing until he flops over onto his belly.

He is now in straight-arm control as described earlier in "Arm upright."

Inverted Wrist Flex

This variation is less stressful on the wrist joint as it forces the suspect straight down onto his belly. Some people find it easier to execute than the wrist twist.

Elements of inverted wrist flex

Instead, use your thumbs...

Your grip on the suspect's hand is the same but don't twist it to the side.

...to push his hand back toward his forearm to painfully stretch his wrist tendons.

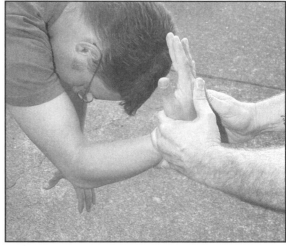

Applications

Grab defense

From a clinch...

...grab the suspect's hand when the opportunity presents itself.

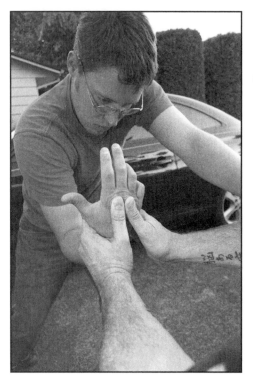

Step back and grasp with your other hand.

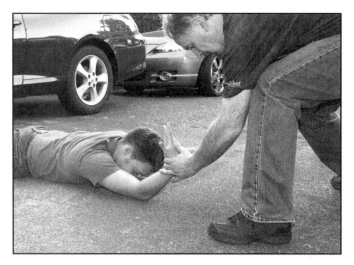

Flex his hand toward him. When he bends forward and steps forward in pain, step back to give him room to sprawl. Keep his arm bent (his forearm about 45 degrees) and don't step back faster than he is moving forward.

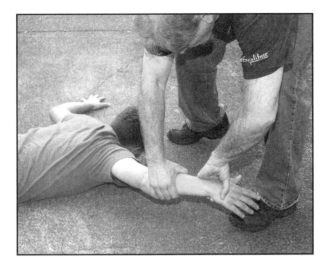

Once he is prone, roll his hand over...

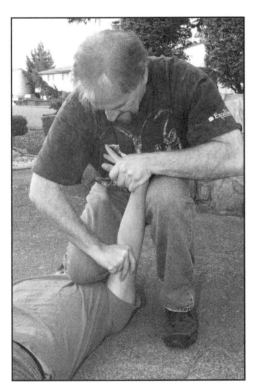

...and lift his arm into straight-arm control.

Out of a car

A suspect grips his steering wheel and refuses to get out of his car.

Secure his left hand and use the knuckles of your other hand to gouge the side of his face (see Chapter 15) to split his thinking.

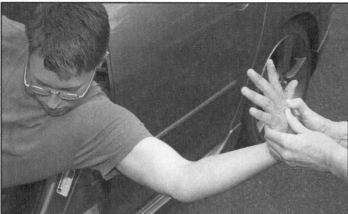

Apply the grip and flex his hand back. Begin pulling him out as you give him verbal commands.

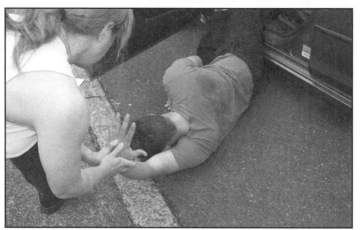

Prone him out.

Wrist Crank

This technique is called sankajo (sahn-kah-joe) in Japanese. It's a powerful move for a variety of situations but unlike most of the other techniques shown in this book it's not as forgiving if you apply it incorrectly. Where his arm is held at a 90 degrees angle, it won't work if it's 80 degrees or 100 degrees. Where his hand is 18 inches from his body, the technique will fail if it's 25 inches or 10 inches from his body. The good news is that it's not difficult to do it right. The secret is – ready? – practice.

Elements of the Wrist Crank

The suspect's arm should be bent 90-degrees.

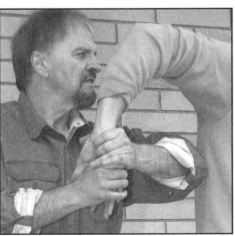

Your hand closest to his body grips the beefy part of his palm and your outside hand twists his fingers. His hand should be open, vertical and held about 18 inches from his side. Stand at his side with your elbow touching his ribs so you can feel him should he try to twist away. If he does, crank the twist harder, maintain the 90-degree bend in his arm, and follow him at his side as you bark commands for him to freeze.

Applications

From minimum custody

Your inside hand presses inside his elbow to bend his arm 90 degrees.

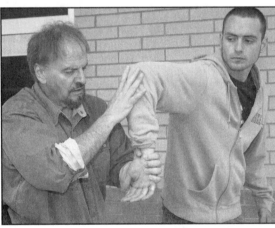

Drop your inside hand to grip the heel portion of his hand as your outside hand holds his elbow in place.

Your outside hand then drops to grip his fingers. To crank on the pain, twist his entire hand toward him. Command him to spread his feet and put his other hand on top of his head.

Note: Think of the process this way: Your right hand grips his wrist, your left hand grips the beefy part of his hand, and then your right hand grips his fingers.

Approach from the front

You can approach the same way from the side and from the rear.

Grab his wrist. Note that your gun side is back and you're slightly to his side, which places you a ways from his free hand.

Step in beside him with a simultaneous bump to his shoulder or upper arm to distract him as you pop his elbow into the 90-degree bend.

Progressively grip his hands as described in "From minimum custody."

How to add a shot of intense pain

When he refuses to obey your commands, give him a shot of intense pain with either one of these techniques.

Pain 1:

Say you have twisted his hand as far as your hands can twist but he still resists. Note how the outside foot is slightly forward. This allows you to apply more pain using your entire body. Maintain a solid grip and rotate your hips toward him so your entire body turns as one unit. Do this slowly because it creates tremendous torque on his wrist joint.

Pain 2: Maintain your grip with your inside hand. Let go with your outside hand, reach through the "window" his arm has formed, and grab a wad of clothing. Simultaneously twist his hand toward his back and pull his clothing toward his chest. Just give him a half second burst then go back to the two-hand grip on his. You lose a little stability with this, so do it quickly and resume your hold.

Pick him up

Sometimes you get a suspect who refuses to get up from the ground. The wrist crank encourages him to see things your way.

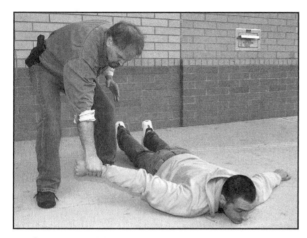

Grab the balking subject's wrist with your outside hand.

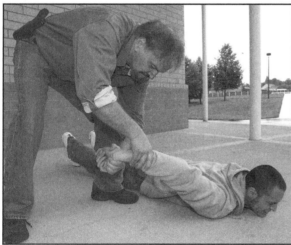

Rotate his wrist so that his palm turns up. Grasp the beefy part of his hand with your inside hand. Don't overlap onto his wrist.

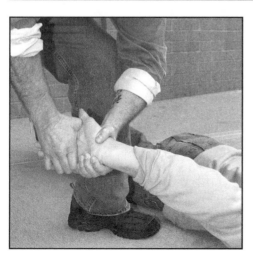

Grasp his fingers with your outside hand.

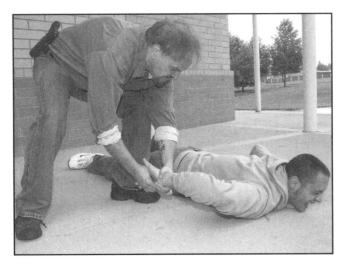

Twist his hand as you push it toward his armpit.

Position his arm at 90 degrees and maintain pressure on his wrist as you command him to stand up.

He stands, deeply ashamed of his crimes.

A fast takedown

You're assuming the wrist crank as shown in the last photo and decide he needs to go down real quick like. Without telegraphing your intentions, step hard to your right and jerk his bent arm straight. Note: This doesn't work well if he is leaning away from you. Yank him when his weight ever so briefly shifts toward you.

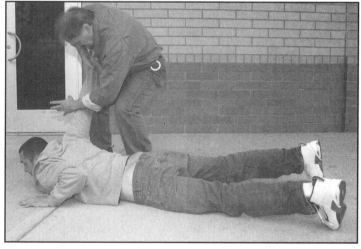

Down he goes. Quickly proceed into any of the control and handcuffing methods shown in this book.

CHAPTER 9

Handcuffing from the wrist crank position

From the standing position...

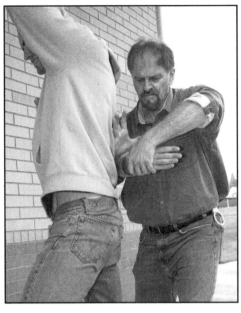

Your inside hand (left in this case) carries his hand to his lower back.

Your outside arm is between his back and arm, and helps push his arm behind him.

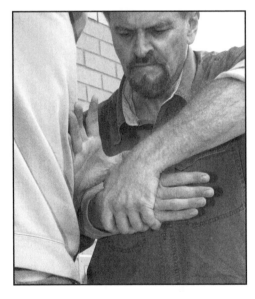

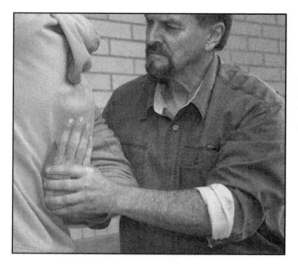

Wrap your right hand over the back of his hand as your left peels off. Then place your left hand over your right and bend his hand toward you.

Pull him back so that he is off balance. Now handcuff.

Wrist techniques are highly relevant to modern police work where quick and low profile compliance is required. I presented several in this chapter but with practice and experimentation, you will find a host of other situations in which to use them. Practice them studiously and make them yours.

Elbow Techniques

Armbar

Most police agencies refer to this technique as an "armbar," though the term can be a little confusing, as some officers believe that the suspect's arm has to be straight. Not so. In fact, the technique works just as well on a bent arm, sometimes better.

The armbar is used more often on *Cops* and other reality-based police shows (ever notice how the bad guys are always shirtless on those programs), because it's a natural move that's easy to remember. But it can be improved upon with attention to detail. For example, one common error is to make the technique a muscle contest. This is fine except when the suspect is stronger. Since you can't always tell by looking how powerful a person is, it's better to use solid technique from the beginning.

Chapter 10

Elements of the Armbar

Straight arm

This is the variation most people think of when considering the armbar.

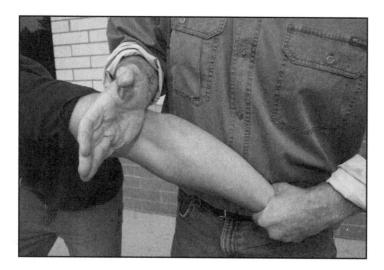

Lift the suspect's arm to and against your midsection, lock his elbow by rotating his arm so that his palm faces upward, and place your wrist against his ulnar nerve, located an inch or two above his elbow. Pressing this hurts a little but the effectiveness of the technique is more about pressing the leverage point.

Pull his hand to your far hip.

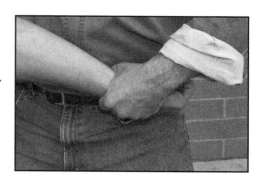

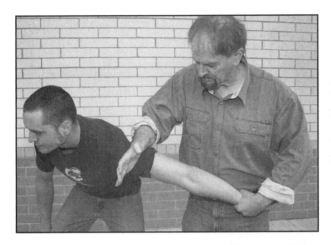

Don't press on the upper arm because you won't get the same leverage benefit as you do pressing on the ulnar point. This makes it easy for the suspect to resist.

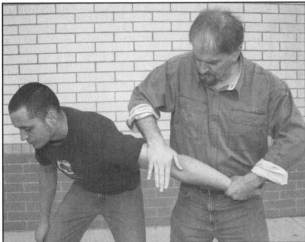

Don't press his ulnar point with your hand because it can easily slip off.

Don't get ahead of the suspect. It weakens the hold and allows him to resist.

We'll look at taking him down in a moment.

Bent arm

Apply this when the suspect resists by jerking his arm upward. Hand placement is the same as with the straight version.

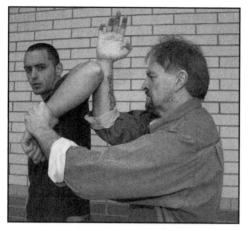

Keep hold of his wrist and press your wrist or forearm an inch or two above his elbow.

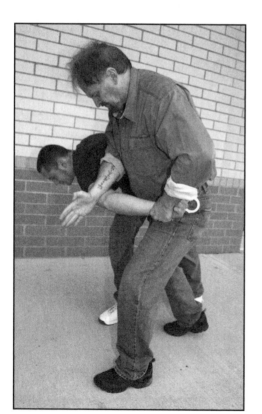

Push his ulnar so his entire arm rolls forward. Sometimes his arm straightens sometimes it doesn't. No Matter.

Take him down in a forward direction as pictured here, or in a circle.

The same elements apply when the suspect is sitting.

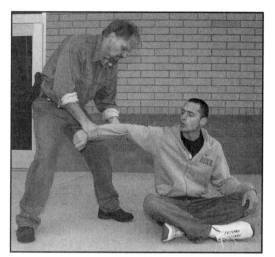

You grab his arm and...

...he resists by jerking his bent arm upward. Place your other wrist just above his elbow joint...

...and press as your pivot him into a partial circle to the ground.

Straight arm when facing the suspect

You often find the opportunity to use this powerful armbar variation when clinching, as a counter, or by lunging forward to grab his arm.

You're clinching with the suspect. When the moment is right...

grab his left wrist with your right hand.

Rotate it...

and press with your upper arm.

Back up as he descends. When he is low enough, it's okay to press with your hand since it won't slip off as easily at this level.

TAKE HIM IN A CIRCLE

When possible, take the suspect down in a circle. To do so, you must pivot 90 degrees to 180 degrees, though occasionally you might have to do 360 or more. I once spun a guy with this technique head first into the side of my police car. In the excitement of defending against his attack with a wine bottle, I forgot that my car was so close. His noggin put a big dent just below the "To serve and protect" logo.

Usually, you circle in the direction of the arm you're holding, but it works the other way, too. If his resistance is strong when you try to take him left, change direction quickly and take him to the right.

Practice, practice and practice until you can do this smoothly.

Other armbars

There are many more armbars in the martial arts world. With the spread of the mixed martial arts, it seems that there is always a new variation appearing on the scene. While this is a good thing in general, they might not all be applicable for law enforcement. Yes, Banger Bob was brought to tears Saturday night on Pay Per View by an armbar his opponent applied after maneuvering BB upside down and turning him inside out. But is it a move for law enforcement?

Can the suspect be handcuffed from it?

If you have to release the hold – any hold - to apply handcuffs, it's not much good for police work. In every defensive tactics class I've taught there is always a young officer, who asks, "How about this technique? It's a killer." Then he leaps into the air and leg scissors his training partner's neck, takes the guy to the floor and pretzels the hapless man's arms and legs into some horrific position from Medieval torture times, then asks in a tone begging for a compliment, "It's a doozie, ain't it?"

"Shore is, yes indeed," I say. Then I burst his bubble. "Now put on the cuffs."

"What?"

That ends that.

However, if you have a doozie of an armbar that you have perfected AND you can handcuff from it AND it falls within the guidelines of your agency, go ahead and add it to your repertoire.

Here are a few scenarios using the armbar and ways to make it more effective.

Applications

When pushed or pulled in all four directions

The suspect can resist in four directions: forward, back, to the far side, and into you. If you're alert, you can apply the armbar as a counter response in each direction. If you're not, you'll have to write a report titled: "How I lost my prisoner."

The straight armbar and the bent armbar work well in these resist situations. Let's use some of both.

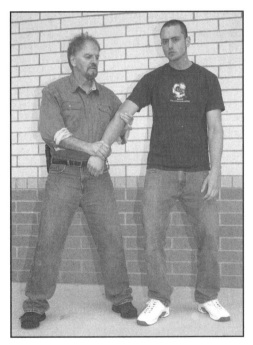

Start from the minimum custody position, as if walking the suspect.

He pushes into you:

When the suspect bangs into you, you must move quickly to take advantage of his momentum. Do three things simultaneously: step back a little with your outside leg, rotate your body in the direction of the push, and slam your arm against his ulnar. In this case, the suspect's arm is bent his arm.

Rotate his palm up and press his ulnar nerve until he goes down.

FLOW

While it's a natural reaction to resist when someone pushes or pulls you, don't. He just might be stronger. Instead, train to yield to the suspect. Whatever direction he wants to go, go with him – and bring a technique with you.

He pulls to the side:

He resists the minimum custody hold by pulling to the other side. Step in the direction he pulls. Stay even with him as you rotate his hand and press his ulnar.

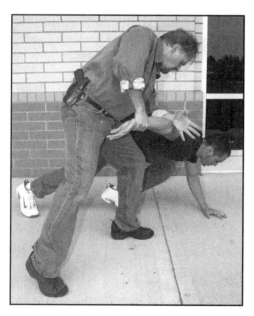

Take him down

He steps back:

You're holding the suspect in minimum custody hold.

He turns quickly in the opposite direction. Follow to stay even with him as you move your arm to press his ulnar.

Press to take him down. [You should be next to the suspect, almost hip to hip. I've moved away from him to show my hand and arm positions.]

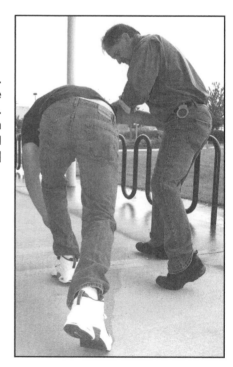

He steps forward:

He steps forward away from your minimum custody. Step quickly to stay with him. Rotate his wrist and press his ulnar.

Turn to take him down.

THE ULNAR

Keep in mind that pressing the ulnar nerve hurts some people, which means it doesn't hurt everyone. No sweat because it's the leverage effect we're after. It's almost a magic button. Press too high or too low on the arm and you just annoy the suspect. Press right on the ulnar point and the leverage effect makes him bend quickly at the waist. Yes, there is the one out of a hundred who won't bend, and we hate him. But most will go down.

Block and armbar

Applying an armbar after blocking a push is relatively easy since the suspect doesn't emit the same energy as he does with a punch. After blocking the punch, consider "softening" (distracting) him with a blow so you can more easily affect the armbar.

Of course, it begs to be asked: is an armbar an appropriate response to a fist assault? Here is my final answer: it depends. There are just too many variables to be conclusive. Elements such as the size and strength of the attacker, your size and strength, the speed and power of the punch, your skill with the armbar, your alertness at that exact moment, the environment, and on and on.

For our purposes here, let's say you deem the situation one in which you can use the armbar. Here is a way to soften and distract the assailant by virtue of startling and hurting him. Unless you accidentally poke his eye, the blow shouldn't be injurious. It's painful, but not scar making.

Block a punch:

The suspect launches a straight-line punch, which you sweep block with your lead hand.

Grab his wrist with your other hand and...

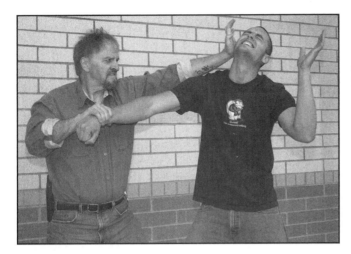

...thrust your palm-heel into his face to distract him.

Rotate his wrist, press his ulnar ...

and take him down.

Two variations for pressing the ulnar

These are painful to some people and less so to others. Use them as a way to deliver a shock of pain to confuse the suspect for a half second before flowing into the regular armbar. If it doesn't work, you're in position to apply the regular armbar.

Heel and knuckle:

You have grasped the suspect's arm and he resists by tightening it.

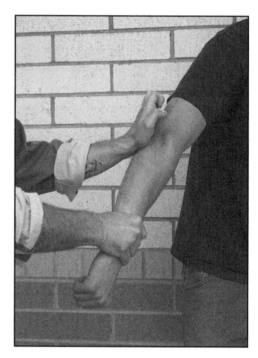

Place the heel of your fist on the suspect's elbow...

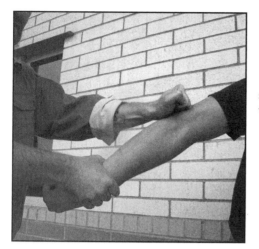

...then rock your fist forward to dig your middle knuckles into his ulnar as you simultaneously jerk his wrist up no more than an inch or two.

If he reacts strongly to the pain, keep on the pressure and pull him to the floor. If he doesn't react, flow into the regular armbar.

TWO ON ONE

You and your partner can both use armbars. It helps if one of you says "Let's take him to the right" so that you don't rip the guy's arms off when you move in opposite directions.

If you're turning him in the direction of the arm you're holding, you must pivot tightly while the other officer steps quickly to keep up. Stay even with each other. If one pushes harder than the other, the weaker one needs to increase his pressure to maintain the integrity of the technique.

Arm rip

The suspect stiffens his arm. Place your wrist on his upper arm and press in.

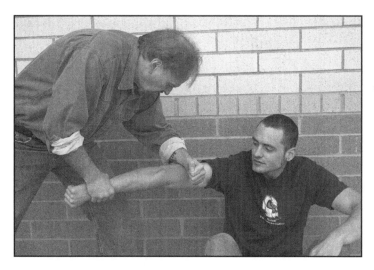

Forcefully rip your wrist down his arm...

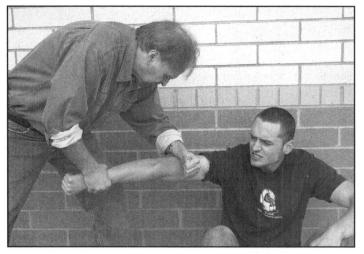

...stopping on his ulnar nerve. Note: As you slide your wrist, simultaneously jerk his wrist up no more than an inch or two. Most react as if shocked.

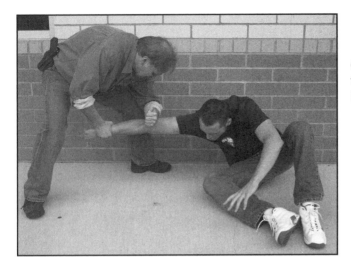

Continue to apply pressure to his ulnar as you pull him...

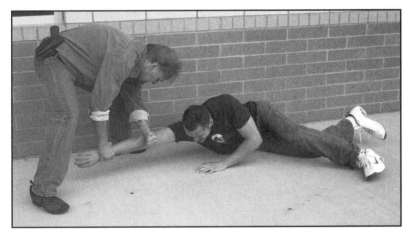

...to the ground.

It's impossible to show all situations in which to use these armbar variations, nor is it necessary. With practice, you will see other opportunities where similar positions present themselves. For example, after practicing the bent arm technique on a seated suspect, as just shown, you will see that same opportunity whether a person is sitting on stairs, a barstool, a motorcycle, a fence, a tree stump, or a little pony. It doesn't matter where and when as long as your position and the suspect's are favorable for the move.

The armbar is applicable to law enforcement. There isn't a great deal of pain associated with it because it's primarily a leverage move as opposed to a pain driven one. This makes it a good technique to use on intoxicated folks and others who are impervious to pain. They might grin and bear it, but they are still going down to the concrete.

Shoulder Locks

This is one of my favorite techniques, although for years my approach had a few flaws. Still, it worked well and allowed me to introduce hard concrete to many feisty folks. Doing it correctly, though, works even better. What a concept! As we proceed, I'll point what I did wrong so you can avoid doing the same.

Elements of the Shoulder Lock

Why it's a lock

Hold your upper arm motionless and rotate your lower arm up...

...to this position. It can't go much past vertical because the joint locks. That's a good thing for us, and a bad thing for the crook.

The steps

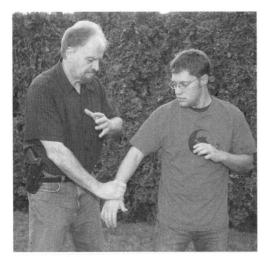

Grab the suspect's right wrist with your right hand.

Slam your left wrist into the crook of his arm, not so hard it knocks his wrist out of your right hand, but enough to remove any rigidity out of his arm.

Simultaneously, push his wrist toward his face as you press into the crook of his arm. The two opposing forces accomplish two things: it makes it difficult for him to resist and it "takes the air out" (free play), making the technique nice and tight.

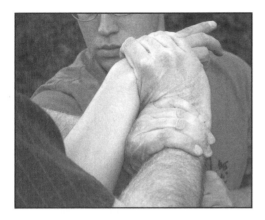

Grasp your lower forearm as you slide your right palm over the back of his hand. I don't find that gripping your arm adds physically to the technique, though it does make you feel stronger, and that's important.

Drop your elbows a little to squeeze out more air. Now do three simultaneous lefts: turn your left foot a little to the left, turn his hand a little to the left, and begin to turn your body to the left. [I'm standing a little farther away from the suspect than you should to show the arm configuration.]

Because he has no way out, he falls...

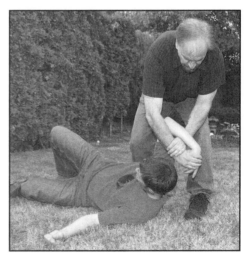

...to the ground.

Here are three common errors:

Don't position his arm with too much play so that he can escape. Take the air out as shown in the third picture. This was my mistake I mentioned earlier. When you achieve a nice airtight hold, you're able to dump people larger than you because you can better apply your body weight to the takedown, rather than pulling with your arms

Don't step outward too far with your left foot. Usually, just rotating your foot in place will suffice. If necessary, step out 12 inches, give or take three inches.

Don't step behind his leg to trip him. He falls just fine without it and you won't have some big lug landing on your knee.

He's down, now what?

This is the same rollover shown in other techniques.

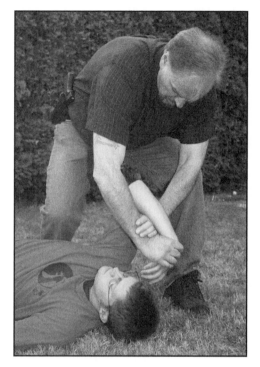

After he's fallen...

...extract your left hand and...

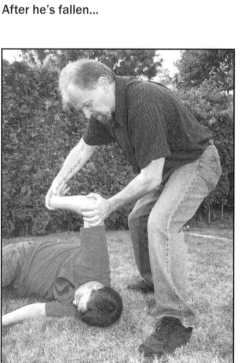

...cup his elbow. Squeeze his palm and elbow toward each other to make him flop over onto his stomach.

Applications

Here are a few situations in which you can use the shoulder lock. Once you begin practicing them, you will discover even more.

From the custody hold

Just as you grip the suspect's arm...

...he pulls away from you. Don't resist, but rather keep hold and...

...drop your wrist into the crook of his elbow as you begin to push his wrist upward.

Lock it...

...and pivot to the left to take him down. [Again, I'm standing farther away than I should so the camera can capture the technique.]

Off a push

This works off of a punch, too, but you must be fast to make it work. A push is usually slower.

Block the suspect's right push with a left sweep.

Replace your left hand with your right and grab his wrist.

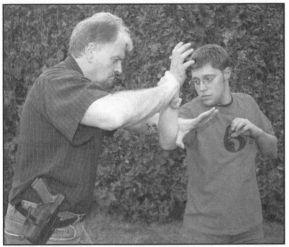

Drop your left wrist into the crook of his arm and push his wrist toward his head.

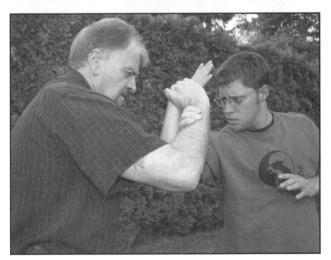

Apply a tight lock and pivot to dump him.

As a Plan B

When another technique fails, look for an opportunity for a shoulder lock.

You're applying a standing wristlock...

...when the suspect manages to pop his elbow up.

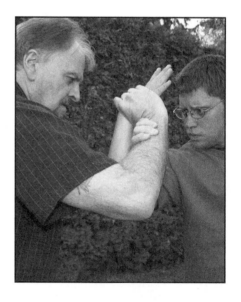

Retain your grip on his hand and slam your left wrist into the crook of his elbow. Push his hand toward his face.

Apply the lock and pivot to take him down.

Bent-Arm Shoulder Torque

This versatile technique works well as a way to hold a suspect in place for a few moments, as a position from which you can handcuff, and as a powerful takedown.

Elements of the Bent-arm Shoulder Torque

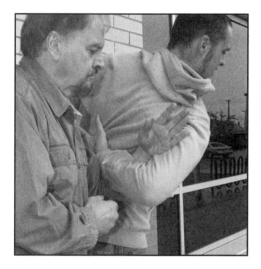

His arm is bent behind him and yours is inserted within it.

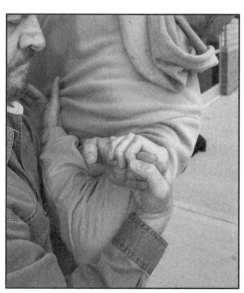

Press the edge of your hand into the leverage point, half way between his shoulder and elbow. Pressing here makes it much easier to bend him and take him down than does pressing near his shoulder or near his elbow.

Chapter 12

To affect pain, lift your left arm to push his hand toward his opposite shoulder, while also pulling his arm away from his back a few inches.

Important:

Don't just push the suspect's hand upward. **Do** pull his arm away from his back, too.

Don't use a weak cupping hand to press into his arm.

Applications

How to enter

Let's look at three ways to get into the bent-arm shoulder torque. As always, experiment to find others.

From the two-arm grip:

This is called "shoot the window."

From the minimum custody hold, the suspect ...   ... resists by jerking his arm upward. See how his arm forms a "window"?

Keep your right hand on his wrist and shoot your left through the opening.

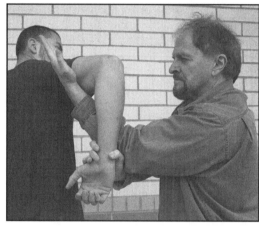

Push his wrist toward his back...

...as you press the edge of your hand into his upper arm, half way between his shoulder and elbow. Release your right-hand and grasp your left hand to assist. If needed, use your upper body, via your upper arm, to push his arm against his back.

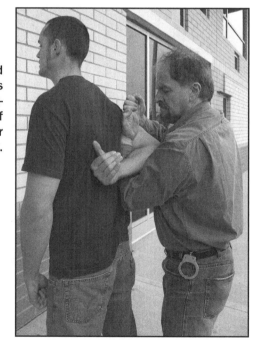

Approach from the front:

You're talking to the suspect and decide to use the bent-arm shoulder torque.

Do three things simultaneously:
1) move toward him at an angle (so that you're away from his left arm
2) gesture with the fingers of your right hand to "come here" (to distract him) and
3) press his wrist back with the back of your hand.

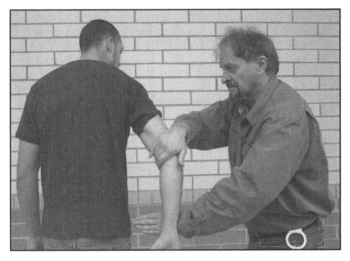

Pull his elbow (to bend his arm) with your other hand.

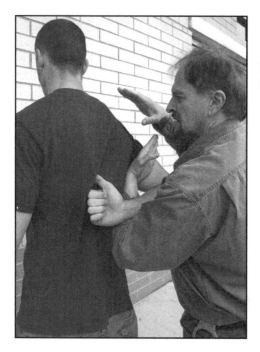

Keep pulling his elbow as your left hand moves from his wrist to his upper arm.

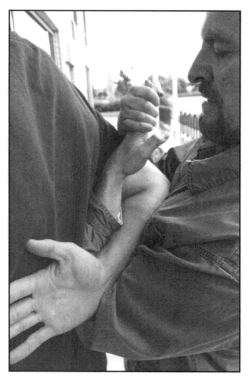

Grasp your left hand to assist, as your upper body pushes his arm against his back. If he requires extra pain, do as described in the last technique: use your left arm to pull his arm away from his back and to push his hand toward his shoulder.

A nifty trick:

This works like a charm but it requires practice. Every time I used it on the street, I would get an amazed look from the suspect.

You move toward his right arm to apply the bent-arm shoulder torque but...

...he is too quick and twists his right side away. By doing so, he inadvertently...

..."offers" his left arm for you. Apply the technique...

...as before. [I'm standing a ways back to show arm positioning. You should really stand just a couple inches away from his back for maximum arm tension.]

Fixing a problem

Don't let the suspect tense his arm in a straight or semi-straight position.

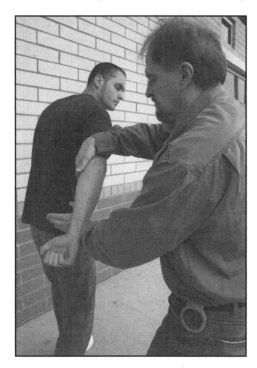

He tenses his arm.

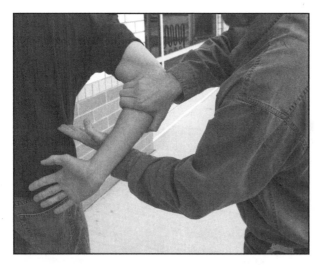

Quickly move your fingers from his elbow to the beefy part of his forearm.

Dig into the muscles and roll them toward you as you simultaneously push his lower arm up with your arm. If he is especially strong, jam your upper body against his arm to push it into his back.

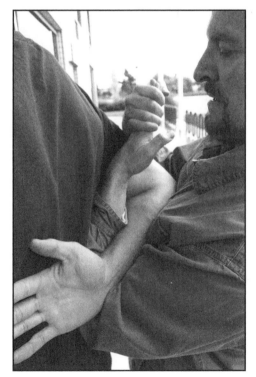

Apply the technique as before.

As a Control Hold

Although the bent-arm shoulder torque is a powerful standing control hold, you might have trouble holding a much larger and stronger suspect. Should that happen, take him down, which we look at in a moment. First, here are three ways to hold him in place.

Grab his other shoulder

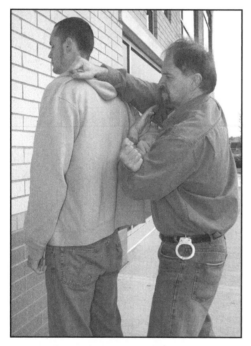

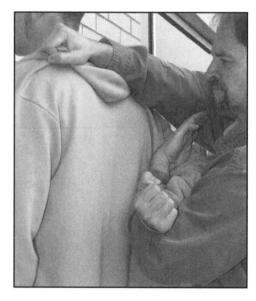

Once you've locked in the hold, grab his left shoulder and pull it back.

Command him to place his hand on top of his head and spread his feet.

Usually this is sufficient to control most people. However, if your suspect needs an extra shot of pain to garner his cooperation, here are two ways to do it.

Chin pull

Once you've locked in the hold, slip your hand under his chin (away from his mouth) ...

...and use the thumb area to hook his jaw and pull it toward you. Don't jerk his chin as that might cause injury. Pull steadily on his chin as you simultaneously lift your left elbow to force his bent arm upward. Order him to stop resisting.

Shoulder press

When you lift the suspect's lower arm, he naturally bends forward to escape the pain. If he bends too far, he might escape the hold. Here is technique to prevent that and to give him a blast of pain at the same time.

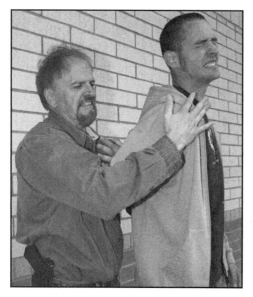

You're cranking on the hold and the suspect starts to bend forward in pain. Slap your palm on the front of his shoulder and pull it back as you lift his bent arm.

Handcuffing Position

With just a couple of minor adjustments, you're ready to handcuff.

Handcuffing

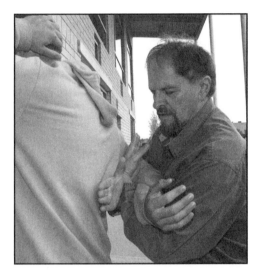 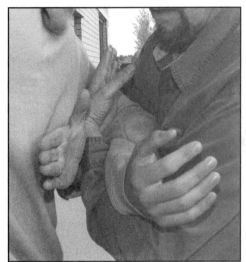

From the hold, begin to slide your right arm between his arm and his back.

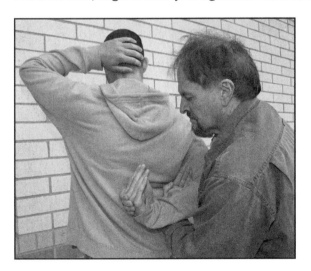 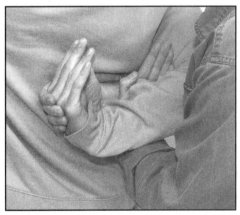

Grasp the back of his hand in a wristlock and...

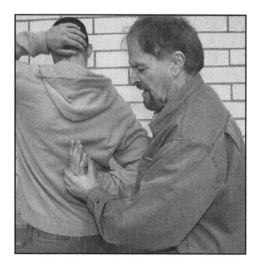

...slip your left hand out.

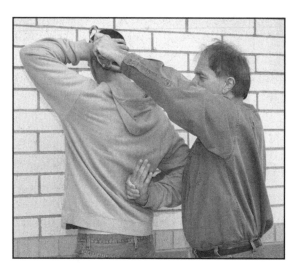

Control him with the wristlock and handcuff when you're ready.

Takedowns

You can execute a takedown in any of the above scenarios. Here is how to do it as a counter when grabbed.

From initial contact

This entire procedure is one continuous motion. Strive for smoothness, not speed.

The suspect reaches toward you. Block his reach with your lower forearm.

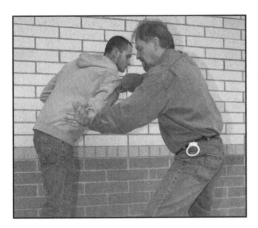

Push his wrist back behind him as you pull on his elbow to bend his arm.

Your right hand now joins your left as you pull. Elevate your left forearm if needed to give him a shot of pain and make it clear what direction you want him to go. Step toward his side a little and begin to move your outside leg behind you. Don't get ahead of him. Stay beside him for maximum power.

Continue to take him down in a circle...

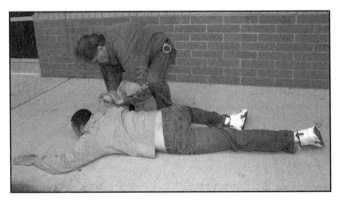

...until he kisses the earth.

Prone Control and Handcuffing

You have some powerful options in this position for controlling and handcuffing.

Without changing your body position: AKA cruel crowbar

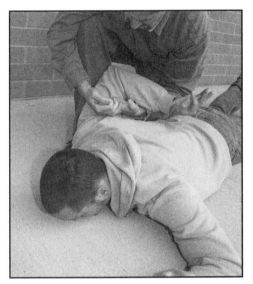

Simultaneously move your right leg up to block the back of his arm so he can't remove it, and then place your palm on the center of his back.

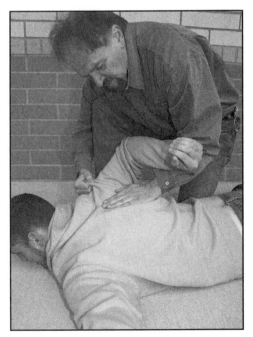

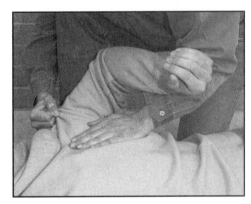

Like a cruel crowbar, lift your elbow, which in turns lifts his arm and sends his shoulder into the red pain zone. Hold him in this position for as long as you want...

Changing your body position

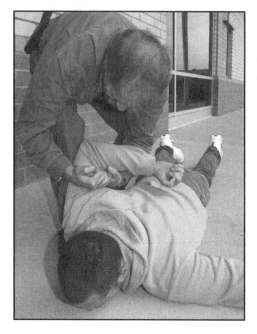

You've taken him down. To move to his front...

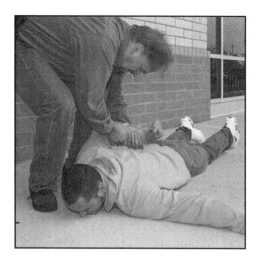

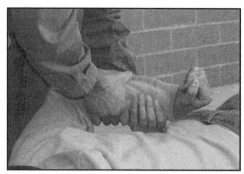

...jam your left shin behind the back of his arm so that he can't escape and grip his arm as shown. Step toward his shoulder with your right foot as you pull his arm upward a little and toward his opposite shoulder. Pulling on his arm keeps his brain preoccupied with pain as you transition. When he is thinking about himself he isn't thinking about you or about escaping.

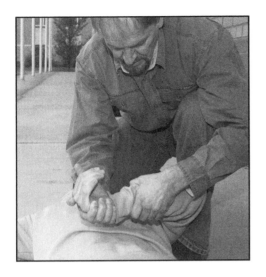

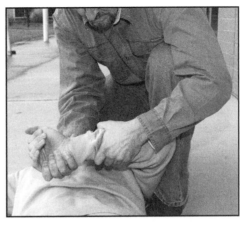

Twist his wrist for additional pain as you talk to calm him.

Drop your knee onto his shoulder, pull up on his arm, and command him to cross his ankles and put his other arm out to the side.

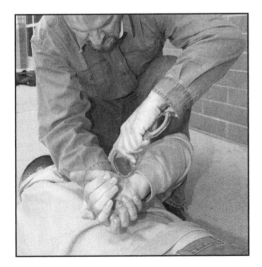

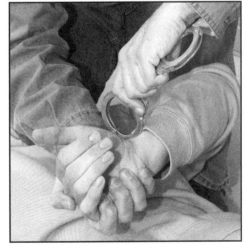

When the moment is right, maintain the twist and arm elevation, and begin cuffing.

Note: As with all techniques, reward the suspect when he cooperates. Reduce the pain, but don't release the hold. He might be faking or he might get feisty again.

Knee Bent-arm Torque

This variation uses your knee instead of your arm as a cruel crowbar. The advantages are that you don't have an arm entangled and the knee makes the technique hurts big time. Proceed slowly because too much force can injure his shoulder. Use this anytime you take the suspect down onto his belly and you have hold of an arm.

Knee torque

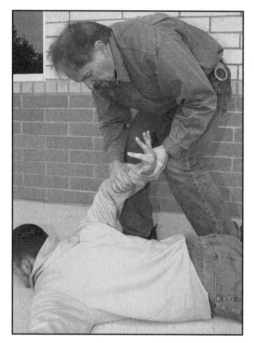

You've taken the suspect down. Lift his arm up high enough...

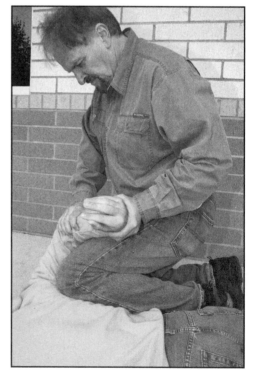

...to drop your knee into his shoulder just above his armpit. Notice how the thigh slopes downward. Place your other knee on the ground.

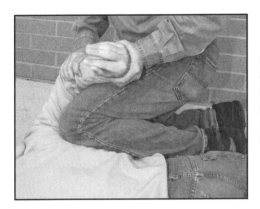

Push his arm slowly down your sloped thigh. Jamming it down forcefully can injure him. Restrain him in this position until your backup arrives. Let's say you don't have backup and you want to proceed with cuffing.

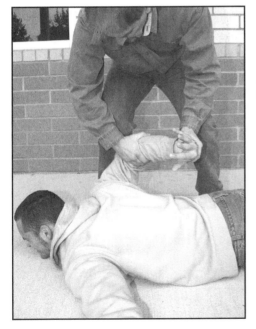

Jam the back of his arm first with your right shin...

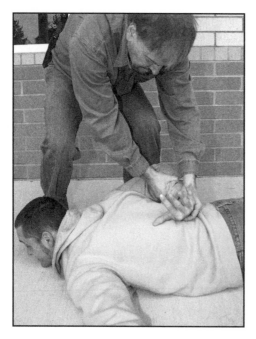

...then jam it with your left shin as you move around to his shoulder. Change hand positions as you did in the last technique, maintaining continuous upward pressure on his arm as you do so.

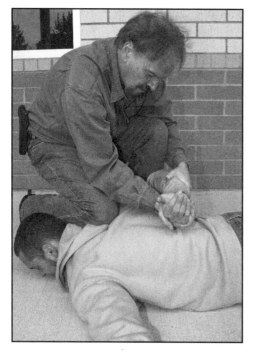

Drop your knee onto his shoulder. Cuff.

Hitting

Citizens don't like to see you hitting people, the chief's office doesn't like hearing about it, and neither do your immediate supervisors. What about the media? You bet your spit-shined shoes they love it. A citizen hits you and no one cares. But should you hit him back, it's almost a requirement in the cosmos that someone nearby captures the moment on a cell phone camera. That person then scampers to a television station and within an hour a spray-haired and Botoxed news person breathlessly announces, "Captured on tape. The film the police don't want you to see. See it tonight at five." Of course, they don't just show it 5 o'clock; they show it ad nauseam for days after.

Although hitting never looks good, when you're confronting a suspect who wants to send you to the hospital or the morgue, you gotta do what you gotta do to get home.

So here's the plan. Do everything possible not to hit. But if you gotta, here's how.

Hands

It's common knowledge these days in martial arts circles that hitting the head with the fist can injure said fist. So here is the rule on that: Don't do it.

While punching people in the face doesn't look good PR-wise and it gets complaints, you can sweat those things out. But a broken hand can have a profound effect on the rest of your contact with the suspect. Should your punch not stop his aggression and he reaches for a weapon, but you just shattered your weapon hand on his jaw, things could get ugly.

During my 25-year career, I punched a hold-up man who was throwing a series of jabs at me and an arrestee who managed to pull my partner's gun partially out of his holster. I was fortunate that these blows didn't injure my hand and I subsequently got these people under control using joint manipulation.

The third time I used my fist was when the suspect, as if he were in a Hercules movie, picked up my 200-pound partner and tossed him through the air. I punched the guy and, for the next three weeks, the guys at the precinct all wanted to write crude things on my cast.

Here's the thing: My fist was about two inches from the guy's skull when, I swear it's true, I heard that buzzer sound that TV game shows use when the contestant makes an error: *rrrrrrrrr*! It even sounds a little like the word "error." But before my brain registered the last "r," my knuckle had disintegrated to dust.

Here are a few ways to avoid hearing that buzzer.

Chapter 13

Elements of Hand Striking

When to hit

The usual motivations:

- To get a suspect to release a weapon.

- To distract.

- To "soften" him so you can better apply a control hold.

- To knock him away from you, from someone else, or from a weapon.

The improper way

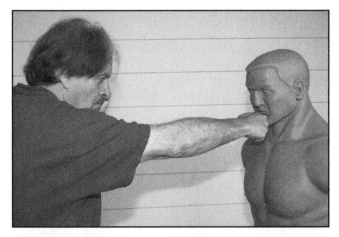

Punching the jawbone, a structure similar in hardness to a horseshoe, can break your fingers and knuckles.

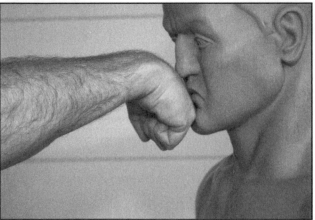

Hitting at an off angle risks spraining or breaking your wrist.

The better way: the palm-heel strike

The palm-heel is cushiony and supported by the wrist and forearm. Some teachers say to hit with the entire palm but I've found that tends to tweak my wrist, too.

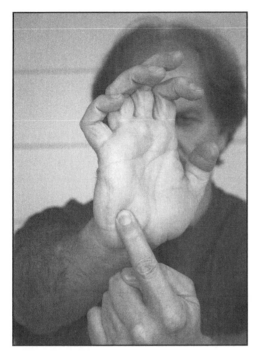

But if you rotate your hand a little toward the little finger side of your heel, your hand is more solid, the impact area more concentrated, and the blow is still supported by your wrist and forearm.

Fist and Palm-heel Targets

I live in the Pacific Northwest where nine months out of the year people wear sweatshirts and coats, a well-padded exterior that can make hitting the upper body a wasted effort. Just try to penetrate a heavy sweatshirt over a heavy shirt, or a heavy winter coat – forgetaboutit. One of our narc officers shot a man wearing a heavy winter coat with a .25 auto and the round didn't penetrate the material. I don't know many humans who can hit harder than a .25 round. Therefore, hit these targets.

Head

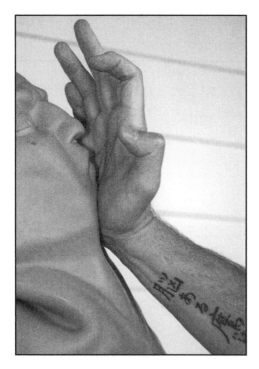

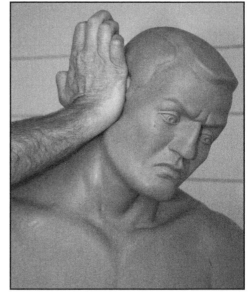

Ear: hit to jar the head and affect disorientation.

Jaw: hit to jar the head, affect disorientation, or to push the head back.

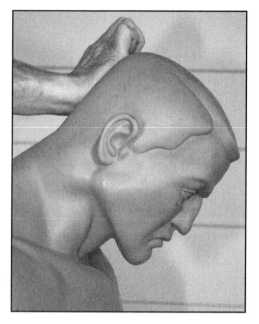

Back of the head: hit to jar and affect disorientation.

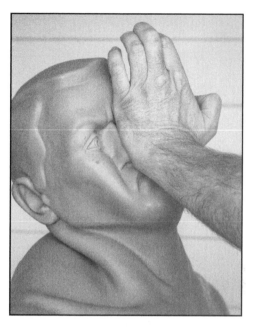

Nose: hit to affect pain and momentary blindness due to tearing.

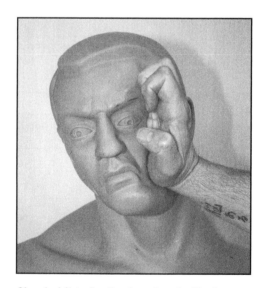

Cheek: hit to jar the head and affect disorientation.

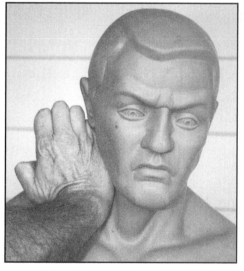

Neck: (**Warning**: dangerous target) hit to jar the head and affect disorientation.

Arms, shoulders

Shoulder: minor pain, effective for turning the suspect

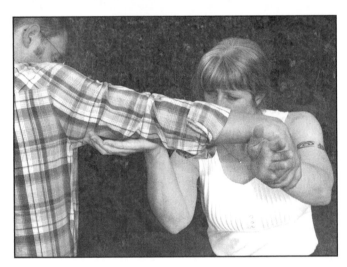

Elbow: major pain and likely injury.

Body

As mentioned, hit the body only when the suspect is wearing light clothing: t-shirt, thin shirt, or tank top. If you've had training, use your fist; if not, use your palm.

Solar plexus: hit to stun and knock the wind out of him.

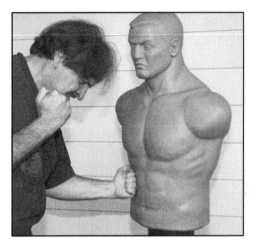

Under the bottom rib: hit to stun and knock the wind out of him.

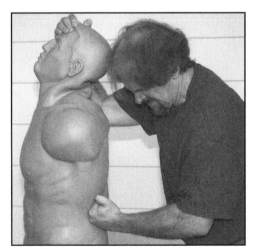

Kidney: hit to stun and affect pain.

Bladder: Fist only; Hit to affect excruciating pain and debilitation.

Groin: Hit to affect excruciating pain and debilitation.

Lower body

It's better to kick the legs than to hit them but if a hand strike is all the situation allows you to do, strike these targets. Use your fist.

Leg connection point: Hit to affect excruciating pain.

Peroneal nerve: pain and debilitation.

Inside thigh: pain and debilitation. Any place inside the thigh will cause pain but two inches above the knee often causes debilitation.

Calf: Pain and possible debilitation.

Applications

Gun retention

When the suspect grabs your gun, cap it with your hand.

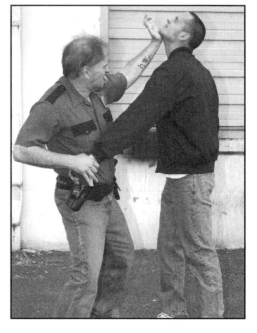

Palm-heel strike his chin multiple times until he releases your weapon.

War story: When I was a rookie, two other officers and I were fighting four suspects in a dinky jail elevator. Three of them were putting up intense resistance while the fourth was fighting like a caged animal. At one point during the confusion of shouting, cursing, flailing arms and kicking legs, I saw my opportunity to punch a calf that lay stretched (and might I add: begging for it) along the elevator floor. I drove my fist into it with all the zeal I could muster; the scream that pierced through all the other noise indicated I had done well. At least until the elevator door opened and everyone spilled out into the hall. Everyone except for one guy, my partner, who lay draped half way out of the elevator moaning and clutching his lower leg. He had to cancel his three-day hunting trip and has yet to forgive me.

Shirt grab

Drive your fist down into his bladder...

The suspect grabs your shirt and starts to
pull you into him.

...then slam your palm into his jaw.

Suspect pulls your head down

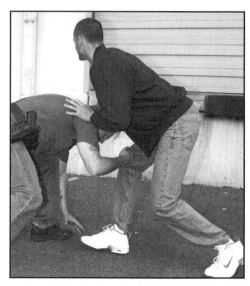

...slam your fist into the inside of his thigh. Hit there again or...

The instant your hand touches the ground...

...ram a punch up into his groin.

Forearm Slams

This is one of my bread-n-butter techniques. Think battering ram but with the side of the ram rather than its end. Here is what makes it effective:

- You can hit with any side of your arm.

- You can hit with a single arm or augment your arm with your other hand.

- The stronger your core – abs, lower back and legs – the harder you hit.

- If you train with bench presses, you hit harder.

- It's a good technique for hitting a specific target, for pushing the suspect, and a good tool to smash through his on-guard stance.

TIPS FOR GREATER IMPACT

- **Tense your six-pack**. When your forearm is about six inches from the target, tense your abdominal muscles hard.

- **Grunt**. Bring it up from deep within your midsection on impact, as opposed to making a sound just in your throat.

- **Drop step**. Take enough weight off your lead foot to advance without lifting it off the floor. When your step concludes, drop your weight hard onto your lead foot while simultaneously landing your forearm strike. The drop step and the strike must be simultaneous for maximum impact.

Elements of the Outside Forearm

Let's begin with the augmented outside forearm slam. You can certainly do it with just the single forearm, and there are times when that is all you can manage, but the augmented version is superior because it incorporates more upper body muscle and allows for some hip rotation into the blow.

From the hands up position...

...position your lead forearm in front of your chest. Place the palm of your other hand just above your wrist, your fingers curled so that they don't extend over the impact area.

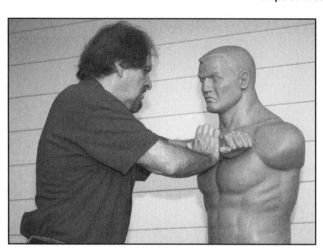

Step toward the target and thrust your forearm forward.

Applications

Here are a few applications. Experiment to find more.

Suspect squares off with you

Lunge forward to strike his arms...

The suspect lifts his arms in a fighter's stance.

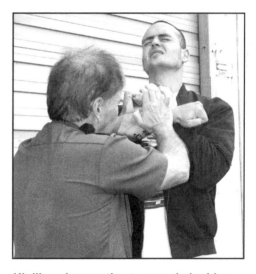

Hit like a locomotive to overwhelm him.

...and smash them against his chest.

Attempted headlock

The suspect lunges high to grab you around the head. Drop low and "load" your forearm...

...and slam it into his ribs.

Training tip: In all of the hitting techniques discussed here and those you devise, practice the blows first. Once you feel comfortable with a hitting technique, proceed with the best follow-up control hold or takedown for the situation.

Weapon retention

The suspect reaches for a weapon. Block his hand and...

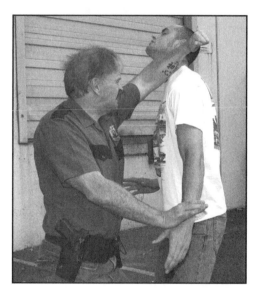

...slam your unsupported forearm into the side of his neck.

Elements of Inside Forearm Strike

This variation involves a swinging whip-like motion as opposed to a thrust. While the outside forearm uses the triceps and chest muscles, this uses the biceps and chest.

From your interview position...

...step forward and a little to the outside with your lead foot, as your rear arm swings out and then hooks back in to strike the target. Think of it as a whip-like action. Hit the target anywhere from your wrist to about mid forearm.

Applications

Here are a few applications. Experiment to find more.

Rib strike to escape

The suspect lunges for your head.

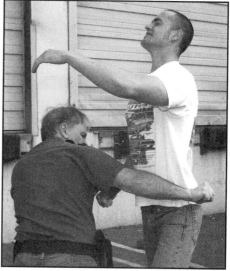

Duck to the side and swing your arm out...

...and into the suspect's lower ribs, or farther back into his kidneys.

Side-by-side defense against a grab for your weapon

You're walking the suspect...

...when he reaches back for your weapon. Cover his grabbing hand with yours so he can't remove it and...

...whip your forearm up between his legs and into his groin. Repeat until he removes his offending hand.

Clinch defense against a weapon grab

Immediately cover his hand and press down hard to keep it in place. (With some holsters, knocking his hand away might dislodge the gun) Shoot your other arm out behind his head (as if punching someone behind him)...

You're clinching with the suspect when he grabs your weapon.

...and then snap it back forcefully to smash your forearm into the back of his neck or head. You can also hit with the thumb side of your fist. **Note:** The concept here is not to step back, which might unholster your weapon. Instead, you must respond counter intuitively by remaining in place and hitting.

Block and counter

Block the suspect's haymaker.

Check his free arm as you step to the side with your rear foot.

Your blocking arm is in position to drive down hard to deliver a stunning slam into the side of his neck. Note: there is a great potential for injury when hitting this target hard.

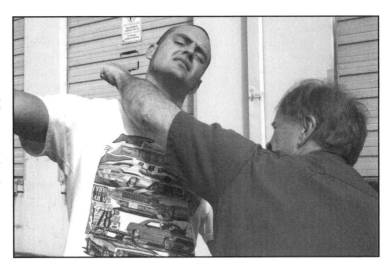

Elbow Strikes

The beauty of hitting with the elbow is that your impact weapon is a hard bone. That means you can hit just about anywhere and the recipient feels it. Now, should you hit his hard skull or his jaw, you're going to feel it, too. So it's better to hit soft with hard, i.e., your hard elbow into the suspect's chest, stomach, forearm, neck, and so on.

One other aspect of elbow striking is that you must be close to deliver it. Kicks are long-range techniques, punches are middle range, elbows and knees are close range, and grappling techniques are super close. I saw a Hong Kong chop-socky flick recently in which the hero dived 15 feet through the air and elbow smashed his opponent in the chops. Don't do that. You might lose your keys.

Elbow strikes happen up close and personal.

- You're in a tight clinch with a suspect and it's not going well.

- The suspect slides up behind you in a crowd and grabs your holstered gun.

- You're thrashing around on the ground with a suspect.

- You're in a close-range situation in which you need to distract or hurt the suspect.

Chapter 15

Elements of Elbow Striking

Keep your hand open when executing elbow strikes to keep your arm muscles relaxed, which increases your speed of delivery.

How many elbow strikes are there?

Picture a big circular clock in front of you hanging in the air. Look at the 6 and then sweep your eyes up the right side to 12, a full 180 degrees, half the circle. Erase the numbers in your mind and mark each degree on the clock from the bottom to the top. Now, think of each mark - 180 of them - as a pathway upon which you execute your elbow strike toward the center of the clock. Actually, when you consider that you can also elbow strike back down the clock, there are really 360 pathways on just one side.

Corn-fused? Check out the pics.

1st-degree path (6 o'clock), striking upward.

From your standard on-guard stance...   ...execute a vertical elbow strike from the bottom of the clock, let's call it the 1st degree...

...up and into the target.

Note: You can deliver all of these strikes with your lead elbow, too.

1st-degree path (back to 6 o'clock), striking downward

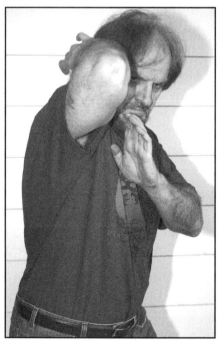

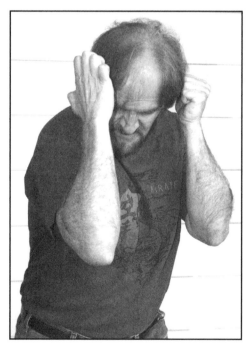

This time, beginning where the last elbow strike ended, strike downward, say to a suspect's hand grabbing your weapon... (Elbows Pic 5)

...and crunch his bones.

Let's jump up to the 90-degree mark, half way up the side of the clock.

90-degree path (3 o'clock), striking inward

Beginning in your on-guard stance...

...swing your elbow around...

...and into the target directly in front of you.

90-degree path (back to 3 o'clock), striking outward

Beginning where the last elbow hit, strike back at someone grabbing you from behind.

The clock concept is simply a device to understand that there are many more angle possibilities with the elbow strike that just the classic up, down, and to the side. So the next time someone from another police agency boasts that his DT program has five elbow strikes you can one-up him with your 360. If you want to include your other arm and the other side of the clock, that's another 360, to total 720 elbow strikes in your DT program. He loses; he buys.

180-degree path (12 o'clock), striking downward

Beginning in your on-guard stance...

...chamber your arm...

... and strike straight down as if hitting a suspect who is tackling you.

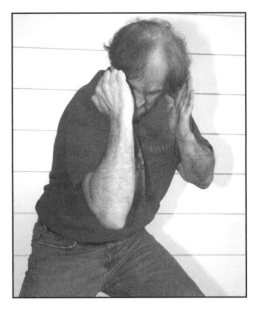

180-degree path, striking upward

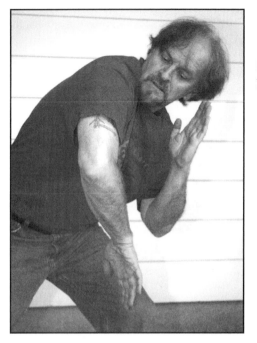

Beginning where the last elbow hit, rotate your arm and ...

...strike straight upward as if hitting someone above you.

Applications

Here are three clinch situations in which an elbow strike works nicely. Remember that a photo is just a captured moment in time. In the case of these scenarios, I chose to strike a highly vulnerable neck, a tender forearm muscle, and a sensitive chest plate. Were they the only targets available? Look for yourself. What other targets are there? When you can see more possibilities, you're thinking the right way.

Gun retention

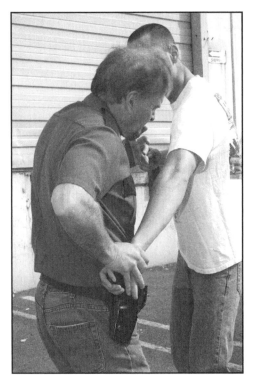

(LEFT) You're clinching with a suspect who reaches for your weapon. Use your closest hand to cap his hand onto your weapon...

(ABOVE) ...and then deliver a horizontal elbow into neck.

Shirt grab

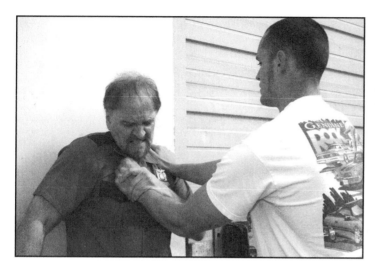

He shoves you against a wall, grabbing your shirt and pinning one of your shoulders.

With your free arm, smash a downward elbow repeatedly into his tender forearm muscles.

Neck pull

The suspect grabs you by the neck.

Time a vertical elbow strike to ram into his chest plate just as he pulls you into him. This target is a thinly covered one even among the obese. If he is wearing a heavy winter coat, strike his chin.

Kicking

Kicking citizens is a public relations nightmare for the front office but, since they aren't on scene to help you when a kick is your best option, let them whine. As always, it's about going home in one piece.

Your legs are your strongest muscles and your shinbone is nearly the equivalent of a steel pipe. When you launch a kick with your big leg muscles and slam your shin into the suspect's leg with all the authority you can muster, you're going to get his attention and just possibly drop him to the floor. If you can manage an immediate second kick to that same spot, you can bet your partner's paycheck that the suspect is going dowwwwwn.

Elements of Kicking

We're only going to use the angled roundhouse. Consider these important points:

Advantage of hitting with the foot: Greater reach

Disadvantages of hitting with the foot: It's easy to sprain your ankle since it doesn't have much support. You can also damage the fragile bones on top of your foot.

Advantages of hitting with your shin: It's a thick, strong bone that hits like a pipe. Aim for soft targets, such as the groin, calf and thigh.

Disadvantages of hitting with the shin: You have to be a foot closer to the suspect. Also, it can be painful to you should you hit the suspect's shin or kneecap.

Chapter 16

Advantages of kicking with the front leg: It's a faster kick because it's closer to the target. There are fewer body moves needed, which increases its speed and element of surprise, and reduces the chance you will lose your balance and fall.

Disadvantages of kicking with the front leg: It's weaker than the rear leg because it travels a shorter distance to the target.

Advantages of kicking with the rear leg: It's more powerful because it requires more body involvement and travels a greater distance to the target.

Disadvantages of kicking with the rear leg: It's slower because it's launched from a greater distance than is the front kick, and it's easy to see coming.

Targets

Groin: This is an overrated target. Yes, it hurts to be hit there in class but out in the real world it receives mixed results. Nonetheless, go for it when it's all that is available but don't stop to see if the suspect drops. If he goes down after your kick, immediately apply a ground control hold. If he doesn't even blink, immediately kick it again or, if the target is no longer available, proceed to another technique. No matter how the suspect reacts, your next move must be immediate.

Peroneal nerve: I accidentally hurt a fellow defensive tactics instructor in class with this and it put him out of commission for a while (and put me on his you-know-what list). Hit the peroneal correctly and your suspect hits the soil, moaning that his leg feels like a giant knot of pain. The P nerve runs the length of the outer thigh along the same line as does the stripe on uniform pants, but it's most susceptible about one third of the way down from where you wear your belt.

Lower inner thigh: Jab your fingertips forcefully into your inner leg about four inches above your knee joint. Now do it again, harder. And again, even harder. And...just kidding. This point hates to be gouged and hit. Some muay Thai fighters (considered by many to possess the most powerful roundhouse kicks in the martial arts) emphasize hitting this target to compress the femoral artery to shock the opponent and weaken his ability to fight. It registers a different pain than does the peroneal nerve strike, but it's often debilitating enough to cause the recipient's leg to fold out from under him.

ANGLE YOUR KICK

Most expert kickers believe that kicking the front of the thigh with a downward angled roundhouse and kicking the back of the leg, the hamstrings, with an upward angle is more effective than hitting these targets on a horizontal plain with a so-called classic roundhouse. Some experts say it's because of the configuration of the muscle fibers on the front and back of the leg, others say it depends on how the recipient places his weight on the legs, and still others say they don't know for sure, but they know it works. I'm in the last group.

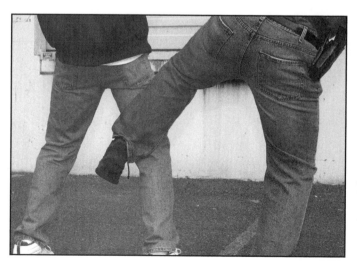

Hamstring: Getting drilled in the hamstring is a weird pain, a cross between a charlie horse and a sensation as if someone just clicked the leg's "delete" button. If the suspect doesn't go down, at least he will be jumping about thinking only of his pain. That's when you rush him. Kick the hamstring with an angled roundhouse.

Front of the thigh: Don't bother kicking here if the suspect is a weightlifter, addicted to all-you-can-eat buffets, mentally deranged, or intoxicated (the peroneal and lower, inner thigh targets work better under these conditions). But if you believe the suspect to be a good candidate for a kick to the front of his thigh, use an upper angled roundhouse.

Applications

Weapon retention

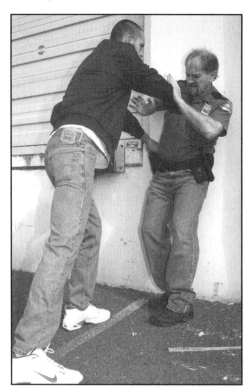

The suspect has pushed you against a wall and is trying to take your weapon.

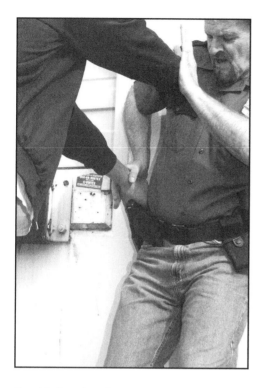

...launch a shin kick into his groin.

Cap his hand and...

When he reacts, peel his hand off carefully to ensure he isn't gripping your weapon and proceed with the best follow-up technique for the moment.

Jab defense

You block the suspect's jab...

...step to the outside and...

...launch an angled roundhouse kick across his thigh.

Suspect reaches for a weapon

When he bends down to pick up a rock...

...you step into range...

...and slam an angled roundhouse kick into his hamstrings.

Suspect assumes a fighting stance

The instant he raises his fists...

...keep your hands in front of you and
launch a hard angled shin kick...

...into his peroneal nerve.

The outcome of a single kick is unpredictable. Therefore, don't kick once and then stand there
looking to see how he reacts. Should he eat the pain and launch into you, you're suddenly
in a defensive mode. Instead, kick him, kick him again if needed, or launch into a different
offensive technique. Keep the heat on him until he's cuffed and stuffed into the backseat of
your car.

Vulnerable Points

Let's define a vulnerable point, to include pressure points, as a susceptible place on the body in which there is a nerve close to a bone. Sometimes these places are called nerve centers, where a nerve branch connects to a major nerve pathway, or where several major nerves join together to form a nerve plexus. I also like to include those places that really, really hurt when poked and gouged just because they are...tender? Okay, that's not scientific but it's nonetheless true. Of course, there are nerves endings involved but not to the same extent as the other more commonly used points. These tender places are simply vulnerable, which makes them applicable to police work.

Get the Point

Pressure point techniques receive mixed reviews from officers for several reasons:

- Not every point works on every person.

- The suspect's state of mind – mental illness, rage, intoxication - affects the technique's success.

- The officer's lack of expertise.

  o He doesn't know the best technique for the situation.

  o He doesn't understanding its goal: give direction, distract, control.

- He expects too much. Perhaps movies and TV programs - like Star Trek and that Vulcan dude, Spock, who could knock folks out with a mere touch - has ingrained delusions of mystical power associated with pressure points.

I've had vulnerable point techniques do exactly what I wanted them to do, and I've had them fail. One night I spent half my shift teaching pressure point techniques to a dozen officers, and then went out to finish the night working patrol. An hour later, dispatch sent me to cover two officers having problems with a resisting suspect. Coincidentally, the two had been in my class.

As we tussled with the guy, I saw an opportunity to apply a pressure point technique. After pressing it for several seconds, the suspect grinned, and said, "Ain't workin' is it?" I lost face and I lost credibility with those smirking officers.

Don't think of these techniques as finishing moves, though there are times they do exactly that. Think of them as supplemental tools that assist and provide that additional nudge you sometimes need to get a suspect to do what you want.

Elements of Pressing Vulnerable Points

Base

Like other techniques in defensive tactics, you need to find or create a base when applying pressure to a vulnerable point. If you don't, the technique won't be as effective as it could be; it might not work at all.

Let's say you're grinding your thumb into a suspect's sinus cavity. If he is standing in the center of the room, he simply leans or steps away from the pressure, leaving you standing there with your thumb hanging out like a hitchhiker; it's a no brainer defense on his part. Therefore, you must create a base so that all the pressure goes into the vulnerable point. You can do that by wrapping your other arm around his head.

When the suspect is lying down, the floor becomes the brace. But if you're wrestling someone on a soft sofa or bed, you need to provide a base, usually with your other arm.

Use more than digital pressure

While some defensive tactics systems use what they call digital pressure to press points, you can use whatever works. Press with your fingers, thumbs, knuckles, elbows, forehead, feet and shins. Your entire body is a weapon. Your police baton, portable radio, pen and your handcuffs work well, too.

While many people think of pressure point control as simply pressing a spot, there are other things you can do. You can:

- press

- rub

- gouge

- hit

- or any combination of the above

A WORD ABOUT PAIN

The philosophy of delivering pain by pressing vulnerable points is no different when applying joint locks or any other type of compliance hold. Your objective is to elicit cooperation, control and/or direct the suspect into a position to be handcuffed. Should you inflict more pain than what is necessary and what the suspect can tolerate, there is a possibility that he will go over the edge. His desperate mind will scream for him to resist harder. He might even experience an adrenaline dump that increases his strength and resistance many times over.

When he does what you want, reduce or stop the pain depending on the situation.

A word about words

The pain from some vulnerable points can confuse the suspect as to what you want him to do. Sometimes this confusion leads to greater resistance. Apply the pain and tell him, "Get down, now!" "Move your arm, now!" or "Stop resisting, now!" When he obeys you, reduce the pressure but maintain the technique in place should he resist again.

Applications

Head

There are several vulnerable locations on the head, primarily because the thin skin there just barely protects the nerves under the skin.

Forehead

This hurts like the dickens.

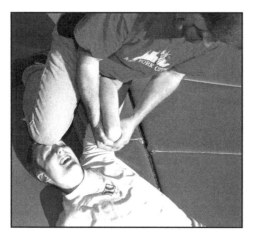

You're applying a control hold on a supine suspect but he is beginning to eat the pain and push himself up. Press your knee down on his forehead to pin him and then rub it in to activate the Pain-o-meter.

Cheekbone

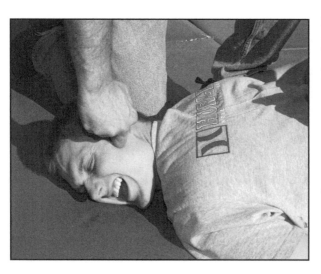

Pressure on the cheek hurts but doesn't give clear direction. Use your verbal commands in conjunction with the technique. "Keep your head down!"

Grind the middle knuckles of your fingers into his cheek.

You can also use this point to assist in taking the subject down.

From behind, place the hard part of your wrist against his cheek and use your other hand to grind in the pressure. Press your head against his to prevent energy bleed. Watch out for his mouth.

Squeeze and command the subject to drop to the ground. Execute the takedown quickly so that he can't flail too much or reach back for your weapon.

Lower yourself to one knee. Brace his head against your body as you continue to press into his cheek. Grab his arm.

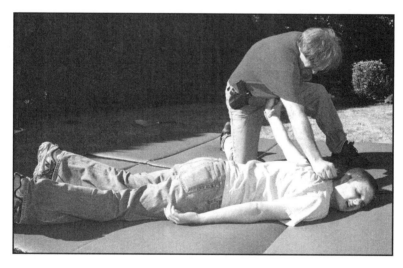

Pull his left arm toward you a little and use your pressing arm to nudge him onto his stomach. Handcuff.

On top of the nose

The nose is a highly vulnerable facial feature. Even the toughest brutes tear up, which interferes with their vision. Use this on a seated subject or on a standing one, as long as he isn't too much taller than you.

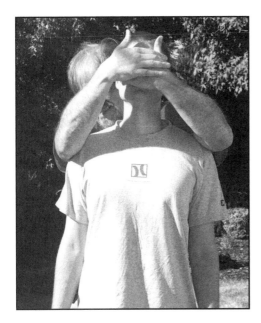 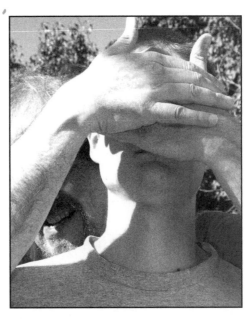

From behind, cross your hands over his face...   ...and lower them until your palm is on the bridge of his nose.

Lower your forearms and press your hands into his nose until his head is against your upper body.

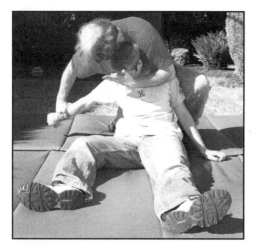

Inflate your chest as you grind in your palm, and lower him and yourself to the floor. You don't have to drop your knee to the floor but most people find they have better control when they do. Lean him back a little so he ties up his hands supporting himself. Grab his right one. Push his nose to the right and...

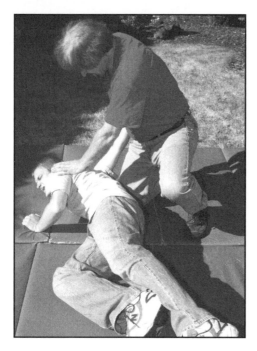

...flip him over onto his belly for handcuffing.

Under the nose

Known as the infra orbital nerve, pressure on it is painful and gives clear direction. Use it to "help" people out of a chair, up off the floor, or backwards off a barstool. Watch out for their germy mouths.

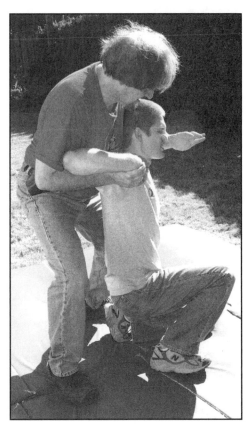

To pick up a seated resister, use the cartilage on the thumb-side of your wrist...

...to press into the nerve point and lift.

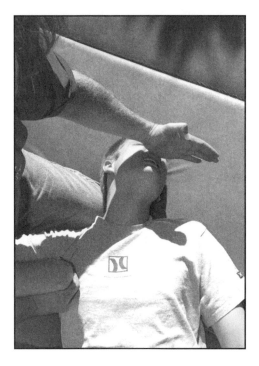 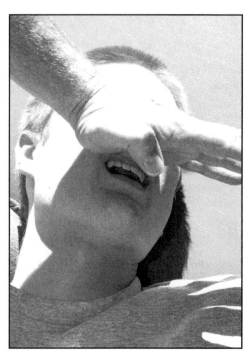

You can also use it to hold a subject down. Rub it a little to intensify the pain.

Neck area

This old classic delivers gagging discomfort while giving direction. Brace the subject's head with your arm or use the floor.

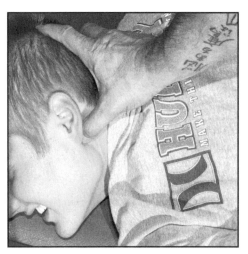

Find the hollow under his ear. When he yelps, "Ow! That's my mandibular angle," you've got the right spot. Grind your finger or thumb into it.

Hands and Arms

The arms and hands offer a number of vulnerable points, some painful, others intensely so.

Hands

Sometimes a motorist won't let go of the steering wheel. The wheel creates a base.

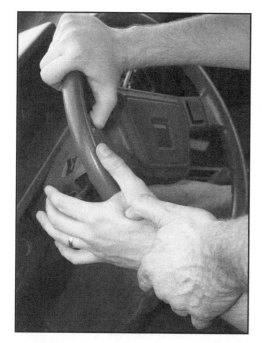

Use your knuckle or thumb to grind into the web on the back of the hand.

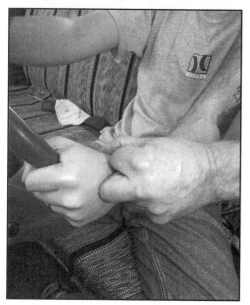

Use a knuckle to grind into the fine bones on the back of his hand.

 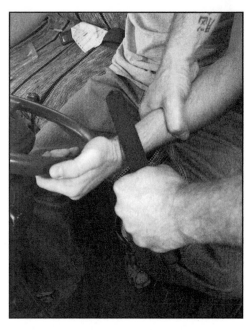

Use the end of your baton to grind into his hand.

Strike the radial to force him to release his grip.

Forearm

Pressing these points gets mixed results. Imagine a large letter "V," its point beginning at the inside of the elbow, its sides extending diagonally two inches outward.

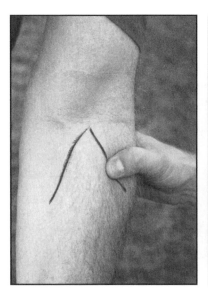 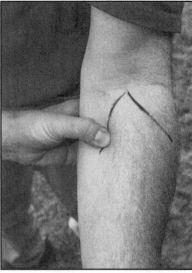

Gouge and rub one or both of these points.

Biceps

The tender muscles on the front of the arms are vulnerable to heavy pressure, especially when braced. Only do this when a partner holds his other arm.

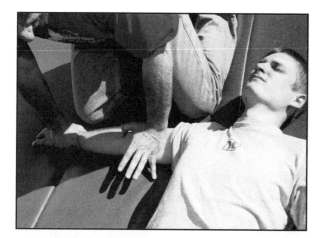

Lean on his wrist and use the edge of your other hand to saw into his biceps.

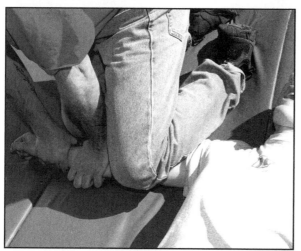

Use your knee or shinbone to saw his biceps.

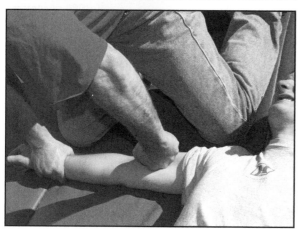

Drive your fist into his biceps.

Triceps

While the big muscles on the back of the arm aren't as sensitive as the biceps, most people feel a hard press there combined with a sawing motion.

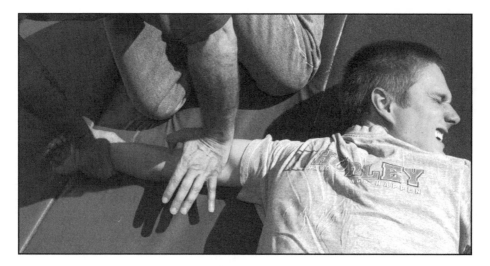

Use the edge of your hand to press and saw.

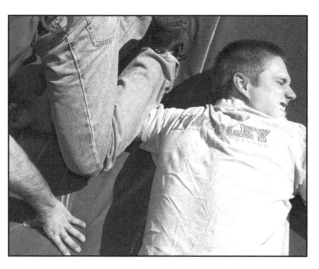

Do the same with your shinbone.

Torso

Chest plate

Pressing this highly vulnerable target hurts and it restrains.

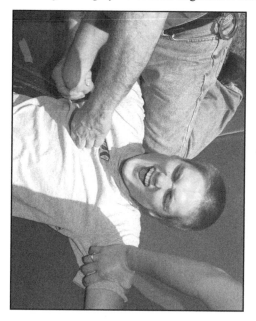

You and your partner struggle to restrain a supine suspect. When he starts to sit up, place your middle knuckle between his pectorals and lean your weight into his chest. Your elbow point works well, too.

Bladder

Pressure here is strangely miserable.

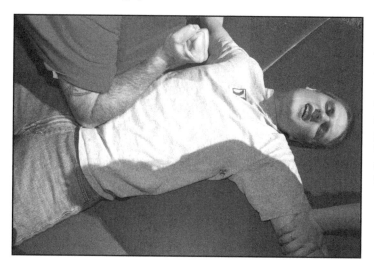

Your partners are controlling his arms. Use your fist or your elbow to dig down and at an angle toward his privates. Lean your weight into it and rub an inch or so back and forth.

Legs

Inner thigh

Aim for the femoral nerve motor point, four or five inches above the knee on the inside. Some call the pain "goosy," which pretty much nails it.

As your partner controls an arm, grab a thrashing leg and press your knee into the point. Wiggle it in to get his attention as you command him to stop resisting.

Outer thigh

The common peroneal on the outside of the thigh, just under the stripe on your uniform pants, is a debilitating target to strike, as we discuss in Chapter 16, but hard to press since it's rarely positioned correctly.

Shinbone

Pressure here makes most suspects comply with lots of heavy whimpering. Use your baton.

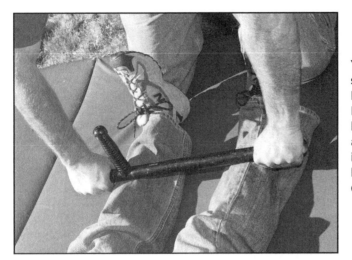

Your partners restrain the suspect in the supine, but he continues to kick. Press your baton across both shins at any point and lean your weight into it. For added pain, roll the baton an inch or so in each direction.

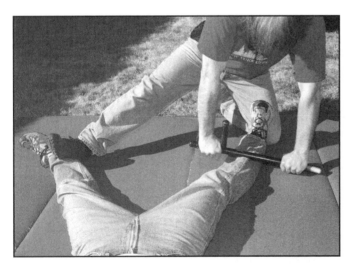

You can apply pressure to one leg, but you must figure out a way to trap his other.

Calf

If you get a subject who can tolerate this one, run for the hills. I've had people confess to crimes they did 30 years earlier. One involved a chicken, but never mind that now.

Your partners are controlling the subject's arms but he is still kicking and trying to get up. Press your baton across both calves, lean your weight into it and roll an inch in each direction.

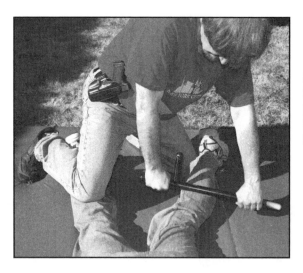

It works on one calf too, but you have to control the other leg. Try pushing it out to the side and leaning your knee into the calf belly (the widest part) of that one.

Head and Neck

In all my martial arts books and DVDs, I emphasize easy techniques and simple concepts and principles. If you ask a question in class and your teacher gives you a complex answer, he is trying to be impressive or he is missing the point of hand-to-hand combat. Fighting is too fast and furious to be complicated. Never is this more important than when thrashing about with a combative suspect.

In this section, we look at ways to control the suspect's head. The concept is this: Control his head and his body follows.

We are also going to look at ways to make him sleep when other options are not feasible. The concept is this: Put him to sleep and his body snoozes too.

Head Disorientation

We see our world through our eyes (you can quote me if you want). The ground is down there, the ceiling or sky is up there, and everything to the right is, well, to the right. When we look up or in any direction, we most often do it on our own accord. Since we control the action, there are no perceptual issues. However, when someone else forcefully turns or lifts our head, we experience a brief sense of disorientation, dizziness, and sometimes confusion that gives us pause. That is what you want to force upon a dangerous suspect so that it provides you with a window of opportunity to dump him, apply a control hold, and handcuff him. Since you don't know how long that window is going to be open, you must act fast.

Here are a few situations in which you force the window open.

Defense/Offense

Palm forehead

This move always works like a charm for me. To get a sense of what it feels like, look at this page for a moment and then quickly snap your head up so that your face is flush with the ceiling. Did you experience a mild sense of dizziness? Well, it's worse when someone forces your head up and continues to force it back until you splatter onto your back.

Swat aside the suspect's reach.

Lunge forward with your other hand and palm his forehead back.

Continue to push so that his face looks straight up as you move even with him. Keep pushing as he goes down.

Grab his arm and proceed with a turnover technique.

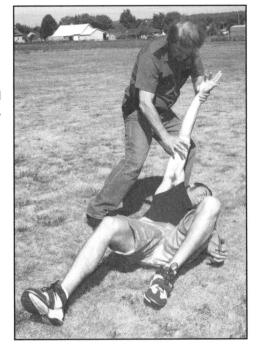

Elbow-hook forehead

The suspect's disorientation here is similar to what he felt in "Palm forehead." This is my favorite Plan B technique when others fall apart. **Note:** A common error is to stop walking as soon as the suspect bends backwards. This allows him to step back and catch his balance. Keep walking until he plops onto his back.

You're applying a wristlock but he begins defeat it.

Release the hold with your right hand and shoot your arm toward his head.

Hook the suspect's forehead with the inside of your elbow. Walk past him allowing your hook to bowl him over.

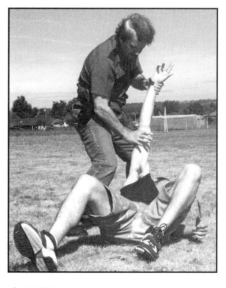

Grab his arm and quickly roll him over.

Head-tuck takedown

The disorientation aspect here isn't as intense as in the first two techniques, but it's enough to make the takedown portion work well. **Warning**: There is potential for injury when stretching the neck forward, especially when done explosively.

When the moment is right, cup the back of his head with one or both hands and pull his head down...

You're clinching with the suspect.

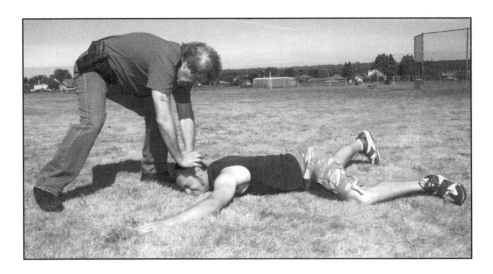

...and continue in one continuous move until he becomes one with the lawn.

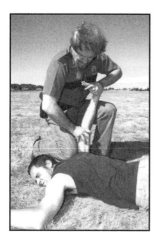

Apply an armlock and proceed with cuffing.

HEAD TWISTING CAUTION

Whenever you twist someone's head there is risk to that person's neck. It's critical that you strive for a smooth and methodical twist as opposed to an explosive one. Young recruits and hardened martial artists can tolerate these techniques in training (most of the time) but that might not be the case with the average street thug. Now is the time to consider under what conditions you would use such force, or not use it. For example:

• If you're quick to lose your temper: No.

• Against an armed suspect: Yes.

• Against a teen acting like a jerk: No.

• Against an elderly person: No.

• Against a superior fighter: Yes.

Head twist takedown

This move is powerfully disorientating: first you force his head to his right, then to his left and then you spin him. But use caution. An explosive twist might result in serious injury.

A suspect lunges forward, his left arm extended.

Simultaneously catch his left arm at the elbow and cup his neck with your other hand.

Do three moves simultaneously: Step slightly to the left, begin to pull his arm downward, and push his neck down and to your left. His face now looks to your left.

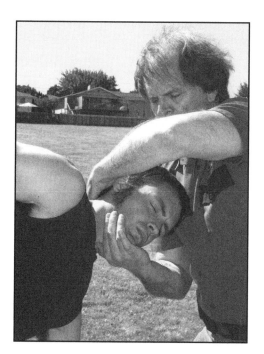

Slide your right hand off his arm, grab his chin with it...

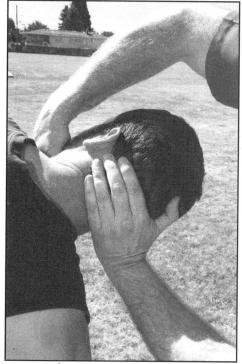

...and then twist his head in the other direction, to your right.

...he easily falls onto his back

Step to the left to take him off balance as you continue to twist his head so that by the time his face is looking skyward...

Immediately grab an arm and commence to apply a control hold.

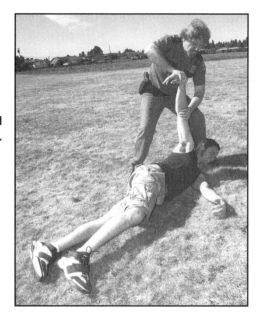

Note: Strive for smoothness in execution as you transition the suspect's face from down, to left, to right, and then straight up. Smoothness of delivery is sufficient to disorientate the suspect and is much safer on his neck than is great speed and power. The weakness in this technique is that you don't have control of his arm when he falls. Be mindful of that and grab it the instant he lands and is still somewhat confused.

Carotid Constraint: Sleeper Holds

Many police agencies have banned sleeper holds from their defensive tactics programs. Nonetheless, it's important that officers know how to apply these simple techniques should they encounter a suspect who cannot be controlled through normal pain compliance holds, there are insufficient officers on the scene to restrain him by sheer numbers, baton strikes and Tazer hits are ineffective, and the environment is not conducive to using a firearm.

Sleeper Hold and Carotid Constriction Hold Defined

Sleeper hold

A sleeper hold occurs when there is constriction, roughly 11 pounds of force - against one or both carotid neck arteries. When conditions are perfect (like that would ever happen), he goes to sleep in four to ten seconds.

Choke hold

A choke hold occurs when about 33 pounds of pressure is applied against the front of the throat, specifically the trachea, with the forearm, shin bone or baton. Unconsciousness takes up to 2 ½ minutes. That's dangerously too long considering that the violent suspect will continue to fight until he finally goes to sleep.

Use When There are no Other Options

I was the first to teach carotid constriction on my department and it didn't take long before I saw officers applying it on suspects when other tactics would have worked as well. There were three reasons for this:

1) I taught them that it was a completely safe technique, which at the time we all thought was true. Although it has proved to be safe in martial arts schools where there are rules, tap outs, mats and well-conditioned athletes, these elements don't exist in the harsh realty of the street. Violent people high on drugs, booze, rage, or mentally deranged, don't tap out and are seldom well-conditioned athletes.

2) It's a simple gross motor technique. Those officers who, for whatever reason, didn't train sufficiently in the many defensive tactics techniques that were taught, naturally fell back on those moves that were simple to use and had a history of working well, such as the carotid constriction hold: Slip your arm around the perp's neck, squeeze, and lower him to the floor. Case closed. Or rather, eyes closed.

3) Some officers found it empowering: "You failed the attitude test and now I must put you to sleep."

At this writing, the carotid constriction hold has never killed anyone in training or in martial arts competition, but it has killed people in police work. Yes, there were extenuating circumstances in these cases – violent drug overdoses and excessive resistance that led to neck injury – but the fact remains that people died.

Therefore, it's good policy not to use carotid constriction on a violent person when a lesser level of force would be effective in controlling him. Now, some officers will read the last sentence, and argue, "It is a lesser level of force." I sort of agree, at least when life is fair, the sun is just-right warm, birds sing a happy melody and never dump on your windshield. But we all know from police work that life is seldom fair.

The bottom line

When you're about to do battle with a violent suspect and any technique other than the sleeper hold suffices, use it. However, when you deem that a situation warrants greater force, and you choose the carotid constriction sleeper hold with full knowledge of the risks, it's good to know how to do it.

Elements of Getting Behind the Suspect

Since few suspects stand motionless as you move behind them, let's examine a few ways to force your way there.

Approach unaware

This generally occurs when you come upon the suspect in the process of attacking another person: You walk in on a husband beating his wife; you come upon a street person assaulting someone; a motorist outside of his car lunges for a weapon on his seat.

You come upon a man attacking a woman in a car.

Grab him from behind...

...and apply the sleeper.

Off of a punch or push

The key with this technique is to push the suspect's upper arm. Because of that hinge in his elbow, pushing his forearm won't turn him, but pushing his upper arm will since it's closer to his mass.

The suspect pushes.

Block with your hands or arms, one hand pushing his upper arm to start him turning.

Quickly step behind him and apply the hold.

Free tip: When pushing his upper arm, he will spin like a top or barely move. Since you can't tell how rooted a person is, train to always move behind him as he turns.

Take advantage of his distraction

Push it forcefully to turn him and begin to step behind him.

The suspect turns slightly for whatever reason, which gives you an opportunity to push his upper arm.

Since your pushing arm is close, slip it around his neck. If for some reason you can't constrict with that arm, simply use your other.

When he kicks

While martial artists train constantly to block kicks, it isn't difficult, especially an untrained kick. Now, I'm not minimizing the danger when someone launches their foot at you, but pointing out that it's arguably easier to knock aside a leg than a much smaller arm that is faster and more versatile angle-wise.

Your task isn't to stop the kick but to knock it aside, a move that is almost a natural reflex. I've had first-day students do it automatically. So let's take this natural reaction, add a couple of elements to save your fingers, and get you behind the kicker.

Straight-line kick:

The suspect launches a straight-line front kick. Swat it aside...

...with your wrists hard enough...

...to turn the suspect's body.

Move in quickly and insert your arm for the sleeper.

Note: Angle your blocking hands so your fingers are safely out of the way. This protects your digits so that you can type, shoot and count.

Circular kick:

The suspect throws a circular kick at you.

Swat it aside with your wrists . . .

to turn his body.

Move toward his back for the sleeper.

Forceful shoulder twist

This is a favorite among many police officers because it's an easy-to-do gross motor movement and because the opportunities to use it are many. Actually, feel free to use it anytime you need to get behind a suspect in a hurry.

Straight twist:

You're talking with a suspect and decide to take him into custody. When the moment is right - he is distracted, he blinks, he is speaking or listening to you – thrust both hands quickly toward his shoulders.

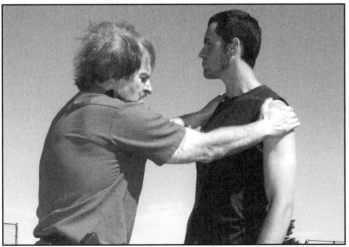

It doesn't make a big difference which shoulder you push and which one you shove, although it's generally easier to push the farthest one and pull the closest.

Push/pull hard as you step around the shoulder you're pulling.

Slip your arm around his neck and whisper, "Sweet dreams."

Free tip: Whenever executing the shoulder twist, your initial move must explode fast and hard without hesitation. Your fast-acting brain process looks like this: decidetomoveMOVE!

Chest slap and twist:

This is a great –make-'em-jump technique. First, you startle him and then take advantage of the moment. It doesn't hurt, although for an instant he might think it does.

When you deem the moment right as you're talking to the suspect...

...launch a slap...

...into his upper chest. The suddenness of your movement and the hollow sound emanating from his chest startles him...

...long enough for you to apply the push/pull and apply the sleeper.

Shoulder-tuck takedown

Sometimes your swat block is so powerful or it catches him just so that it twists him around, causing him to lean back toward you off balance. Life is good. Take advantage of the open window and dump him on the ground.

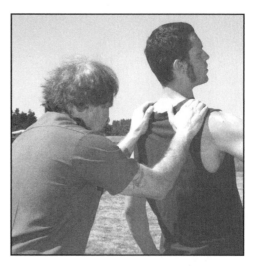

Place both hands on his shoulders...

...and, pointing your elbows down, jerk him to the ground.

Slip your arm around his neck for the constriction.

Elements of the Sleeper

The common carotid artery supplies the head and neck with oxygenated blood. The arteries begin at the heart and travel upward along each side of the neck. When constricted, the blood supply is slowed – not stopped as is often believed. While all the techniques shown here apply pressure against both arteries, pressure against only one works, too. When it's applied perfectly, the suspect loses consciousness in a few seconds.

Note in the photo that the elbow is centered under the suspect's jaw which allows your biceps and your forearm to constict the neck.

DON'T DO THIS

You've wrapped your arm around a suspect's neck in the standing position and then you've stepped back to take him down. For just a moment, maybe 3 to 5 seconds, you're dangling much of this guy's body weight from the crook of your arm and by any existing fragility in his neck. You're a living noose. The situation is worse should the suspect resist violently. This can be flat out dangerous to the suspect (and to officers in training) and is an invitation to a lawsuit.

Don't let the person dangle from your arm for several seconds. Take him straight down fast, one second max.

Applications

There are many variations of the sleeper hold but let's not complicate the subject. Once you get behind the suspect, whether standing or sitting, use one of the following.

Basic constriction when standing

It's difficult to get a tight constriction on a standing suspect, at least not as tight as can be achieved on a person positioned lower than you. Here is a way to constrict the suspect's arteries while lowering him to a better position.

You push/pull his shoulders

Slip your arm around his neck. Center your elbow under his chin so you can apply pressure on both sides of his neck, not on his trachea.

Wrap your other hand around your fist and push to constrict. As you push, imagine that you're a nutcracker as your elbows move a few inches toward each other to maximize the pressure on the sides of his neck.

Two takedowns

Knee collapse:

This technique can jeopardize your balance so make sure you're in a strong position before you lift your foot off the ground.

Put your foot back on the ground and press your elbow downward against his chest...

Once you feel the suspect is vulnerable to your takedown, press your foot behind his knee until his leg collapses.

... until he sits.

On the Ground

Reposition him

If he sprawls onto his back, which happens when you step too far back...

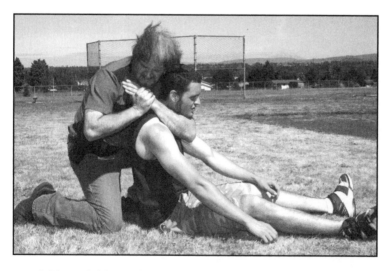

...quickly push him up into a seated position while simultaneously ensuring you have a good squeeze on his neck.

He drops his chin

Should he drop his chin or turn his head to resist you as he lands...

...create an opening to his neck by pulling his hair or slapping his forehead back. Then snugly slip your arm around his neck and put him out.

Option: Place the hard cartilage of your wrist against his nose and clasp your hand with your other. Grind his nose cartilage with vigor. When he lifts his chin in pain, rewrap your arm.

Take the air out (pun intended)

This move is little too subtle to see well in photos.

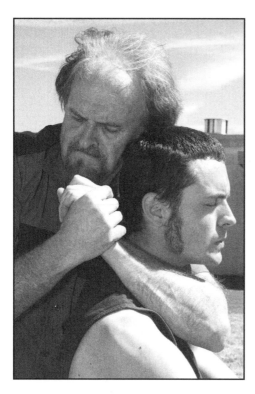

Drop your elbow down his chest and think, "bunch up his shirt," as you press your arm against him, and then pull it up ....

...deep and tight into his neck so that he cannot possibly move. When done right, your training partner will tell you that he can feel the effects of the sleeper even before you start the actual squeeze. (I gave my model a nice squeeze to get the right facial expression from him. It was a chance I was willing to take for you, the reader.)

Head push constriction

The head push described here doesn't facilitate the constriction but it does make for a tight hold. Add this to the "take the air out" technique and the suspect, as my dad used to say, "Ain't going nowhere quick."

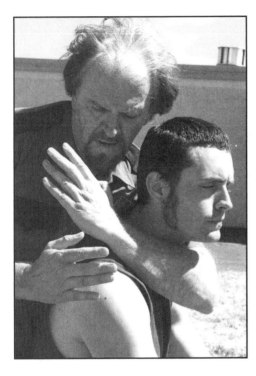

You have wrapped your arm around his neck.

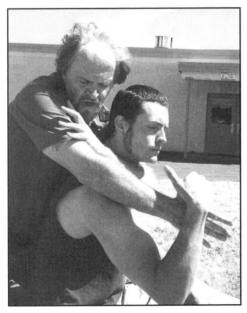

Don't extend your support arm forward because he might grab it.

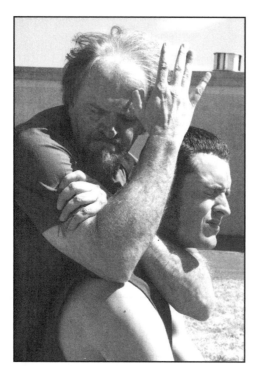

Do stick your arm up as you grab your biceps.

Place your support hand – your palm or the edge of your hand - behind his head. Push his head forward as you squeeze your elbows toward each other.

Ultra constriction

While the head push constriction is tight, this method is tiii-ight! and will likely make the suspect give up his life of crime and do only good deeds forever.

Wrap your arm around his neck, insert your thumb into your armpit . . .

... and grip your biceps.

Move your support arm behind his head, reach as far as you can toward your other shoulder, as you move your elbows toward each other. You might or might not touch your other shoulder; it's the effort that affects the constriction.

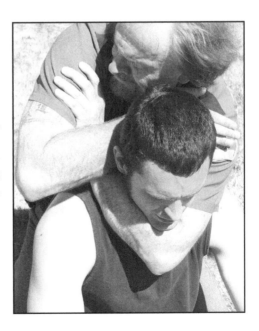

When he goes to sleep

Because you're up close and personal with the suspect, you're going to feel him go limp and maybe hear a string of curse words wind down to silence. When it happens, relax the tension in your arms but don't give up the hold. He might be out for five seconds, 30 seconds, or he just might be tricking you. Some people awaken passive and confused, while others are ready to go another round. Should you disengage from the hold and he springs to his feet like a teenage gymnast, you're back to square one.

Instead, relax the pressure but keep your arms in place until your backup arrives or until you feel the moment is right to do one-handed handcuffing.

Handcuffing

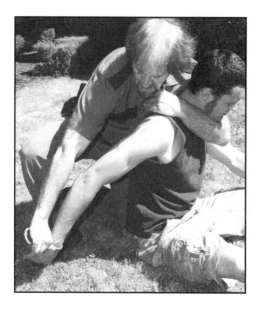

Maintain one arm in place and snap a cuff on his wrist with your other.

Carry that hand behind him as you trap his arm with your leg.

Switch constricting arms and snap the other cuff on his other arm.

Note: Both the seated cuffing and prone cuffing are awkward. Take your time and never give up your neck hold.

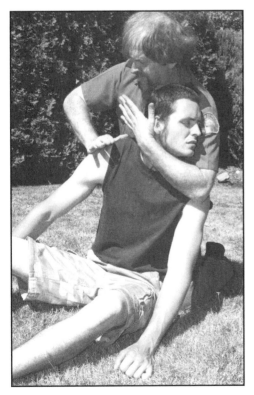

To prone out an unconscious suspect for handcuffing, maintain the constriction and push him over onto his stomach. Protect his face with your hand.

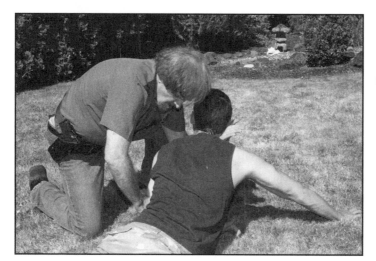

Grab his closest arm...

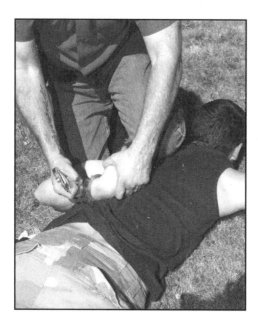

...jam a knee against his triceps, and apply a control. Cuff.

Ground Fighting

Far too many police agencies ignore the issue of ground fighting or if they do mention it, they advise not to do it. Oh, okay. Good advice. Sheesh!

The reality, however, is that ground fighting does happen in police work. How much is hard to say. Research by the Los Angeles Police Department found that more than half of all physical confrontations go to the ground. Writers who sell ground fighting books and DVDs claim 90 percent.

Even if only one goes to the ground every five years, it's a good thing to know what to do once you're there. It hurts to thrash about on the street and sidewalk. Hey, it hurt to pose for these photos! Then factor in the following elements and you have yourself a painful and dangerous grappling environment:

• There is at least one gun present – yours.

• Many suspects would like to take possession of it.

• There is a possibility that friends of the suspect's are nearby just itching to slam a foot into your ribs.

• You could roll out into traffic.

My friend Mark Mireles, a big ol' veteran LAPD cop as well as a grappling expert since the late 1970s, knows the ground well. When he isn't teaching other police officers and mixed martial artists how to make the earth their friend, he is busy bringing home trophies from national and international competition. In the first chapter, Mark shows you powerful techniques for the most common situations that officers find themselves in. In the last chapter in this section, I show a few ways to deal with a suspect when you're down and he's up.

Ground Grappling

By Mark Mireles

Every time a cop hits the street, he never truly knows what's going to happen. Healthy fear keeps him at the ready; it's a key factor in street survival. Cops manage the unknown with physical training, tactical training and the deployment of sound tactics to make a dangerous job a little less so. Think of it this way: good tactics send you home at night in one piece, keep you out of trouble with the brass, and move you toward retirement to collect your pension.

Though you do your best not to go to the ground, fighting is so unpredictable that you might just end up there anyway. It's not a place you want to be foreign territory. The good news is that the unpredictability of ground fighting can be curbed though realistic and practical training.

The Learning Curve

I recall watching a group of academy recruits doing a drill in which one officer engaged in a foot pursuit with another playing the suspect. They ran for about 200 hundred yards, then stopped, quickly put on boxing gloves, and went to fist city at each other. It was clear that many of the recruits had never before fought or at the most had some hand-to-hand combat training. Many were shocked and panic stricken when punched in the face for the first time.

Besides getting their brains rattled a little, these recruits were experiencing fear of the unknown. Fortunately, good training and gifted instructors taught them to anticipate, move, absorb, and counterattack.

Like taking a punch in the face, the only way to learn about ground fighting is to experience it. While there are still defensive tactics courses that overlook this critical phase of officers' training, in recent years many progressive trainers have made strides to address it. The most recent category of defensive tactics training, often dubbed Arrest & Control (ARCON), has incorporated ground fighting tactics as a main block of instruction.

DENIAL

It's unrealistic to think that you can talk everyone into jail; it's never been that way and it never will. At some point, you're going to have to put your hands on people, some of whom will resist. The more complete your training, the less chance for civil liability and a catastrophic injury to you or the suspect. Ground fighting is part of that component. When it happens, will you be ready?

The reality of ground fighting vs. combative sports

Ground fighting in police work isn't Greco-Roman wrestling, judo, Sambo, submission grappling or any other grappling sport that tests your skill under time limits and rules. That said, many of these arts contain technical aspects that apply to the specific needs of real fighting - though they need to be modified. The following techniques are from the art of Brazilian Jiu-Jitsu, coupled with American police defensive tactics, and then designed so that you can control and handcuff a combative suspect in seconds.

Three Types of Suspects

Allow me to generalize a little as I separate the pool of violent suspects into three groups. All three are dangerous and all three can take the fight to the ground.

The Runner

Running is perhaps the most common form of resisting. A runner is usually that person involved in a hand-to-hand drug deal or the one who bails out of a stolen car. The heat shows up and he is off to the races. Sometimes he runs to get away and other times he does it because he is scared. Running adds danger to the situation because when cornered he might fight like a wounded animal, one that takes you to the ground.

The Brawler

A brawler is angry at the world. It doesn't matter who crosses his path, you, his wife, or some poor hapless guy in the wrong place at the wrong time. Whoever it is, the brawler often makes that person the focus of his rage. He is predictable because you know he is going to cause problems, yet he is unpredictable because you don't know to what extent he is going to go off. He might take a couple of swings, and then drop into the fetal position and begin crying. Or he might "go homicidal," taking on all comers. He often appears impervious to pain because of intoxication or mental illness.

The Convict

The third suspect is by far the most dangerous since he might be a sociopath, or close to it. He is often a career criminal and, since you're between him and his freedom, he has made up his mind to kill or maim you. A convict has an institutionalized view of the world. He doesn't care about a uniform, a badge, or a gun; he has nothing to lose. Actually, he has everything to gain: freedom for another day, a week, or six months. He is going to reach into your uniform and see what you're made of.

I once interviewed a convict who used his shackles to choke out a transportation guard on an L.A. freeway. Afterwards, he dashed off to freedom through a residential neighborhood. Two hundred cops and a house-to-house search later, officers found the man hiding in a garage less than a block from where he had left the guard.

The five foot, five inch, 140-pound guy calmly explained that he had nothing personal against the guard; he just saw him as weak. He said that he couldn't live in a cell knowing that he didn't try to escape when it was right there in front of him. What did he have to lose? He was already doing life for violent crimes.

Should you confront such a convict and you're not on your "A" game – you're not trained, alert, aware, or ready – you might not survive your shift.

From the moment of contact all the way to the end, you never know what type of suspect you're dealing with. This is true even when you have dealt with the person many times before. You might go to the ground with the runner, the brawler, or the convict, all of whom can kill you; some plan it and some do it spontaneously. Never underestimate a crook, or anyone for that matter.

Cops Need Ground Fighting

There have been many studies conducted by law enforcement agencies that have examined the dynamics of police officer versus suspect physical altercations. The Los Angeles Police Department conducted a study of use-of-force incidents once and found that over half of all altercations went to the ground. Not all agree with these statistics, but whatever the percentage, it just makes sense to know what you're doing when you're down there. Here are a few factors to consider:

- Most high-risk suspects are ordered into the prone position. Then, at some point, you have to approach the person and physically make contact. The suspect might surprise you with a "Folsom roll," a technique developed in California's Folsom Prison in which the prone suspect rolls away or rolls into you when you kneel on him to apply handcuffs. (Even high school wrestling has several counters for this position.) Ground fighting is a given should this happen.

- You tackle a running suspect and you're likely to go to the ground with him, tumbling, rolling, and wrestling. Ground fighting is a high probability if the suspect doesn't surrender.

- Standing arrest situations can easily end up on the ground. The suspect spins during a pat-down search; he tackles you during the interview; you tackle him; or you trip backing up. Inmates have been filmed practicing many of these situations in prison yards.

- The suspect is a trained martial artist. If he wrestled in high school, he will take you to the ground. If he practiced judo for six months, he might throw you to the ground. Today's younger martial artists take a hybrid approach to their training. They strike and grapple in what has been termed mixed martial arts (MMA). You're likely to go to the ground with these people.

The above examples happen hundreds of time a days in American law enforcement. When I was in the police academy, trainers addressed the subject of ground fighting by simply telling recruits, "No matter what happens, don't go to the ground with the suspect." But tenure and street experience taught me that more often than not the suspect goes down and the officer follows.

GUN! One other significant danger to consider is that in all officer/suspect contacts there is always one weapon present: the cop's gun. Every year, police officers are disarmed and executed with their own service weapons; many of them while ground fighting.

Elements of Ground Fighting

Rule 1: Get him into the prone

Get on top to apply your bodyweight onto the suspect and then do all that you can to get him facing the ground, as opposed to being on his back where he is stronger and more dangerous. Although this might seem like a no brainier, some martial arts disciplines teach their students that the bottom position is a superior place to apply chokes and joint locks. This is reflective of training for sport grappling as opposed to police tactics.

Maneuver him face down and use your weight and balance to keep him there.

Note 1: Always take the suspect down into the prone position to maximize your safety.

Note 2: Control the suspect's hands and maintain control of them until he is handcuffed.

Rule 2: Watch the hands

Hands kill. The hands are the suspect's primary and expedient choice of weapon. If he is armed – and you often don't know - he deploys his weapon with his hands. Whether you work in the inner city, the suburbs, a swanky beach town, or in the country, today's bad guys pack guns, knives, and impact weapons. This becomes an increased factor when ground fighting, since you're in close prominently with the suspect.

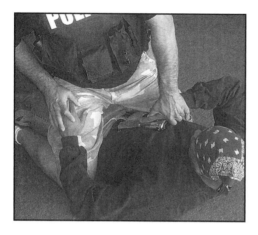

He pulls a gun while supine and in close contact with the officer.

The suspect can use a found weapon in a face-to-face ground fight.

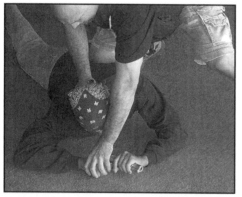

The above threats might still be present when the suspect is prone, but it's harder for him to deploy them, which gives the officer time to react.

The nature of grappling is that one moment you're on top and the next you're on the bottom. That's fine in a martial arts school or in the police academy because you learn from your mistakes. But it's not fine on the street where injury and death await.

There are several positions in which you can find yourself in ground fighting. Let's look at the good, the bad, and the ugly.

Neutral Ground

The following positions and techniques are based on Brazilian jiu-jutsu and have been modified for arrest-and-control defensive tactics. Brazilian jiu-jutsu's simplistic ground fighting functionality is especially applicable to police work.

One-on-one training

As a matter of officer safety, you should always have the strength of numbers when dealing with crooks. When there is one suspect, there should be two officers.

That said, I address ground fighting here from the perspective of one officer and one suspect. A defensive tactics program should start with this model so that the student gets a sound working knowledge of the positions and techniques. Think of these situations as fighting for self-preservation in a worst cast scenario. Once you and your training partners become proficient at one-on-one training, expand it to include teamed ground fighting and dealing with multiple suspects.

The mount

The straddle position uses your body weight to pin the suspect to the ground and then you get control of one arm for handcuffing, then the other.

Mount the suspect. Your knees serve as points of balance.

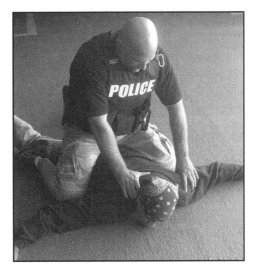

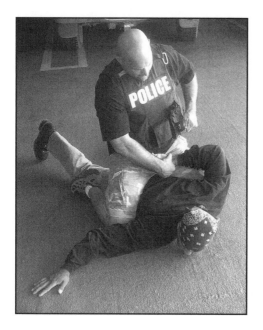 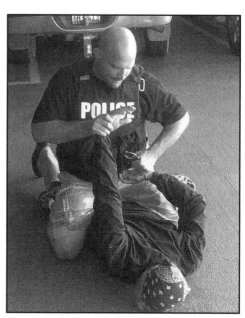

Seize control of the suspect's hands and begin handcuffing.

Note: Straddling a suspect to handcuff is controversial. Try it in your training and explore its strengths and weaknesses.

Mount (prone) resisting/lateral head displacement

Since it's no mystery to the bad guy that your goal is to handcuff him, it's common for him to resist by tucking his arms into his body. He might be attempting to prolong the inevitable or he might be looking for an opening to counterattack.

Don't hit to distract him. I have found that this rarely works because the suspect's adrenaline allows him to absorb a great deal of pain, no matter how many times you hit him in frustration. Instead, displace his head laterally so you can pry his arm away from his body.

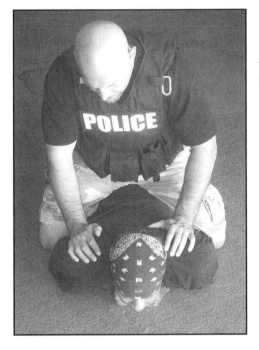

The suspect resists by pulling his arms into his body.

Place your elbow just above his ear and drive his head forcefully to the opposite side.

Reach under his arm and pull his wrist forward. Do this slowly in the event he's holding a weapon.

Pull his arm back. If needed, displace his head to the other side to gain control of the other arm.

Mount knee (prone) on the back control

Place your knee on the suspect's upper back to transition into handcuffing. This is a weighted point of contact that gives you balance and mobility. There are two variations for grabbing the suspect's arm.

Near arm control

This is the most basic and universal method of transition.

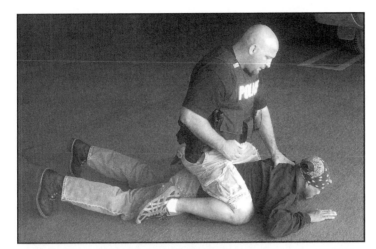

You have secured a mount.

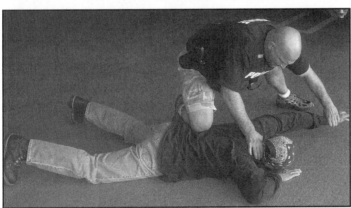

Place your knee on the suspect's back between his shoulder blades.

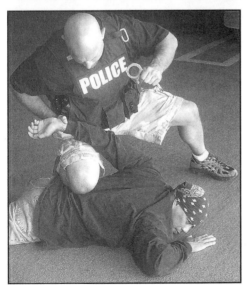

Grab the near arm at the wrist to secure it for handcuffing. Elevating his arm puts great stress on his shoulder joint.

Near arm knee pinch control

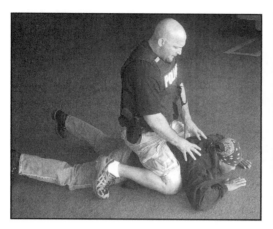

You have a secure mount.

Place a knee on his back and grab his near arm.

Position it between your legs. Note the hand-to-hand position and that the suspect's shoulder is jammed down, which increases tension on his arm and allows you to transition into handcuffing.

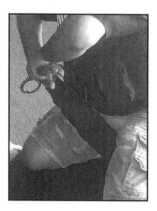

Mount (supine)/crossface leveler

In the struggle to gain control in ground fighting, you might mount the suspect while he is lying on his back (supine). This is dangerous because he can deploy a weapon while facing you or he might try to get yours. Since the longer he is on his back the more chances he has to act, you must immediately turn him over into the prone position. The crossface lever is a painful move that prevents him from thinking about an offensive.

Grab one of the suspect's arms and move it...

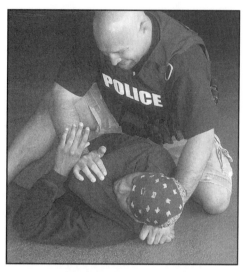

...across his face. Note the position of his raised elbow.

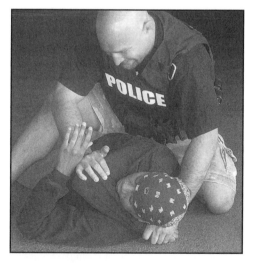

Cup his elbow with one hand and press his arm hard over his face. Reach behind his head and grab his wrist.

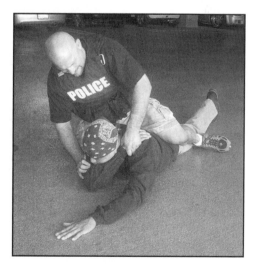

Roll the suspect over by pushing his elbow and pulling his wrist.

Weapon retention

Should the suspect grab your weapon, you must assume he wants to shoot you.

The suspect grabs at your weapon in your holster.

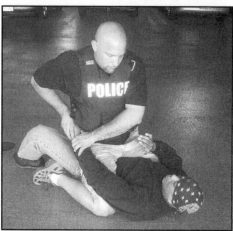

Cup your hands over his, pinning his hand and your gun in place.

Remove your far hand from the weapon, while your other hand continues to cap his grabbing hand. Deliver a hard punch or palm-heel into his face.

Note: Punching someone in the head is always a risk to your fragile hand. Sometimes you do it without a problem and sometimes you break your hand. It's a judgment call. (see *Chapter 13*)

Knee onto stomach and roll over

You're lying chest-to-chest with a face-up subject or you're straddling him as shown in "Weapon retention." Here is a painful way to transition to a better position for you and as a way to roll him over for cuffing.

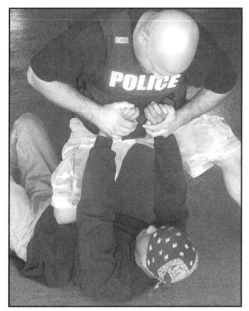

Pop up and drive your knee into the suspect's belly. Use your arms and hands to assist with your balance and control.

Underhook his far arm behind his triceps.

Circle toward his head while pulling on the handcuff.

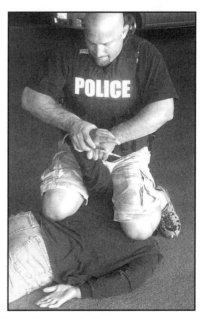

Pinch his arm between your legs and underhook.

North-south control

In the natural dynamics of fighting, you and the suspect might end up in a less than desirable position where you're on top of his head. You must immediately move to get out of biting range and to get control of the suspect.

You're in a north-south position with the suspect.

Push his head away so he can't bite you while simultaneously underhooking his arm.

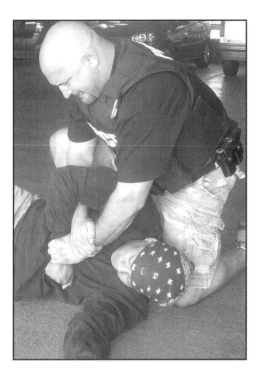

Create a lever with the underhook...

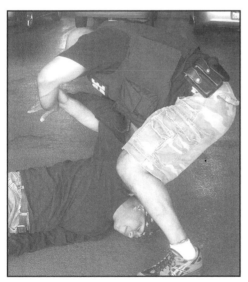

...force him onto his side...

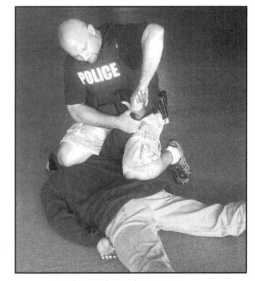

... and over into the prone.

Worst-case Scenarios

The dynamics of fighting are explosive and unpredictable, which are never truer than when ground fighting. Should you get knocked to the ground, you must immediately get back up and engage the suspect. This is easier said than done because he is likely scrambling to get on top of you. You need to buy time, and that is where hip escape, the guard, half-guard, rolls, sweeps, and the check-kick comes into play in officer survival ground fighting.

By no coincidence, worst-case scenario techniques take the most training. Let's get to it.

The hip escape

Brazilian jiu-jitsu fundamentally teaches its students not to rely on muscular strength but rather to become a master of positioning. Think of good position and control as the antithesis of raw muscular power. After all, fighters of small stature founded and developed the ground fighting system into the high art form it is today. This makes it applicable to defensive tactics since cops are big, small, male and female.

Brazilian jiu-jitsu perfected the hip escape. Every law enforcement officer should learn it, as it's a powerful way to escape from a suspect who is on top of you.

The fastest way to learn this technique is to practice the following:

Escape drill

Get onto your back,
knees bent.

Dig your left heel into the ground to straighten your leg as you roll up onto your left side. This action knocks away an attacker who is on top of you (see next sequence).

Repeat on the right side, then back to the left side and continue in this fashion for at least 10 reps

Applied hip escape

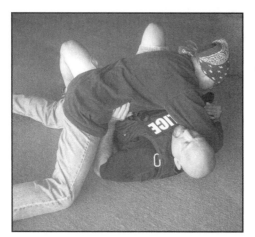

The suspect is lying on top of you.

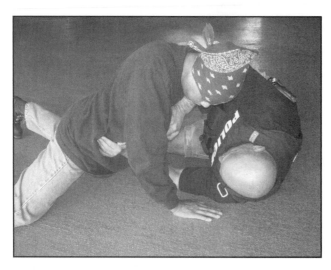

Straighten your legs to create space as you did in the first solo photo in "Escape drill."

You've knocked the suspect off your body and back enough so that he can no longer hold you down.

Post your shin against him and use your arms to push away, all of which help clear your hips so...

...you can get up.

Escape and counter

After successfully using hip escape ...

...roll up onto your knees and begin to reach for his.

Grab behind his knees and pull, as you simultaneously slam your shoulder into his upper body to affect a tackle of sorts to drive him over onto his back. Get back on top and secure a control hold or, get up, back away and draw your weapon.

Hip escape from the mount

You're in the worst combat position possible when the suspect mounts you. You must react quickly.

He mounts you. Immediately thrust your fist into his hips to move him upward.

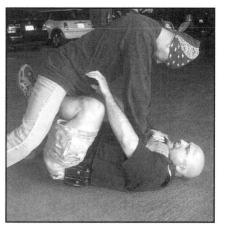

Create space by jamming your bent leg between you and the suspect. Note that your inserted leg removes his body weight from your hands.

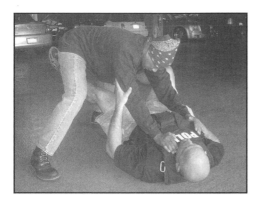

Use your shin – similar to how your legs straighten when using a leg extension machine at the gym - to push the suspect's hips back. It's the action of your leg moving from flexion to extension that creates space.

Push with your left foot to create enough distance for your hip escape. Quickly scramble to your feet.

The Guard

This is a perfect example of where ground fighting and sport blurs. The guard is the cornerstone of effective ground fighting and a defensive position reserved for worst-case scenarios. Many submission sport purists actually like to fight on their backs because they feel they have an advantage over their opponents.

In police work, however, it's a risky situation should you attempt to subdue the suspect by assuming the guard. Under no circumstances should you ever let a suspect get on top of you. You want to be the one on top, in the guard, looking to counterattack. But it happens.

Let's look at three guard positions. They aren't considered counterattacks but rather transitional controls that allow you to launch powerful counters. Notice that in all three, you're controlling the suspect's upper body and hands.

Closed guard

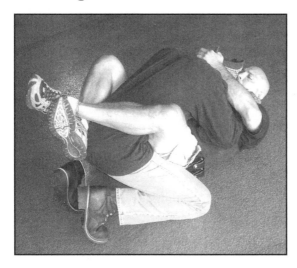

From the closed guard, wrap your legs around the suspect and pull him in tight.

Open guard

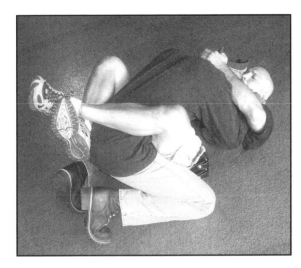

In the open guard, your body is centered on the suspect and your legs are not pinning him.

Spider guard (hooks)

The spider guard is a position from where you can move your feet to the inside of the suspect's legs.

Weapon retention in the guard

Your force options change when the suspect tries to take your life, render you unconscious, or cause you catastrophic injury. Should he have a weapon, it's possible, with training, for you to quickly transition to deadly force on the guard.

Weapon retention from the guard and keylock reversal

The guard position puts your weapon in close proximately to the suspect. If he attempts to grab your gun, you must react immediately.

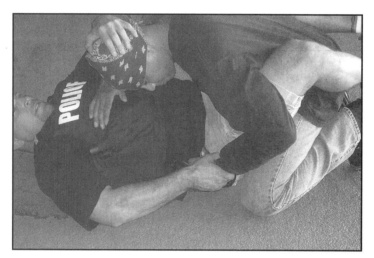

You're in the closed guard when the suspect reaches for your weapon. Cap the weapon, that is, cover his hand with yours, to force it back into the holster.

Apply a keylock hold...

...an intertwined hold where you: 1) grip the suspect's wrist, 2) reach over and then under the suspect's shoulder with your opposite arm, 3) and secure a grip on your own grip.

Crank the keylock behind the suspect's back, and toward his head, to affect tremendous shoulder pain, and to force him off you.

The open guard: check-kick and recover

In the event the suspect hesitates or attempts to follow up his attack with a stomp and kick from a standing position, use the open guard to set up a check-kick to his knee or shin to give him pause so you can get up.

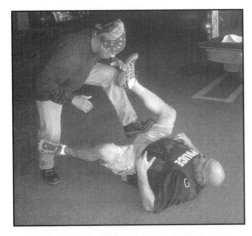

The suspect attempts to stomp you. Check-kick his knee...

...to jam his leg.

Use your other foot to kick his other kneecap.

The half guard

The half guard is a defensive position that allows you to gain control of a suspect who is on top of you by scissoring one his legs with both of yours.

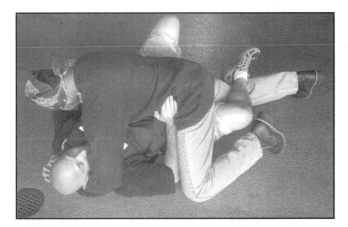

You're in the half guard position.

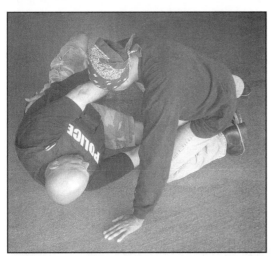

Use the hip escape from the half guard to ...

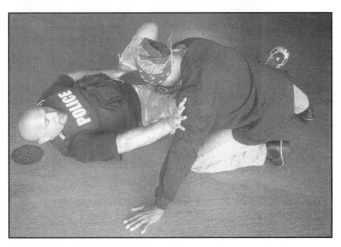

...get away from the suspect.

Rolls

Unless you're a powerlifter, you probably won't be able to bench press a suspect off of you; trying to do so will just waste precious energy. In a desperate ground fight, you need all your strength and wind. The hip escape and the guard are the first steps in economical fighting. The guard is used to set-up rolls and sweeps.

Rolls are effective counters from the various guard positions to get you off your back and on top of the suspect. As you fall, overhook one of the suspect's arms and underhook the other. Then lock your hands together to secure a tight body-to-body position that facilitates your roll.

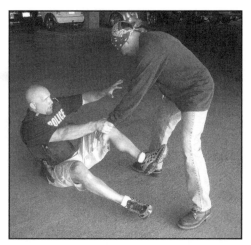

... you trip or he knocks you down.

You're clinching with the suspect when...

When he moves in on you, use spider guard to raise the suspect legs as you apply the over-under position with your arms to....

...raise the suspect in the air.

Use a corkscrewing motion to throw him off to the side and onto his back.

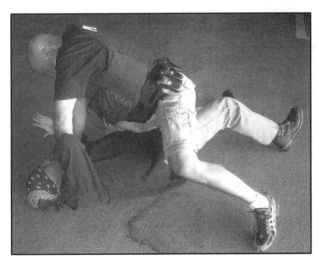

Mount him to gain control or jump back and draw your weapon.

Roll when mounted

The suspect mounts you with plans to rain punches into your face. You must immediately gain control of his hands by capping his fist or grabbing onto his wrist.

The suspect punches.

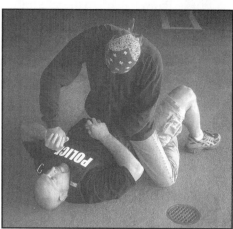

Block or grab his fist and then...

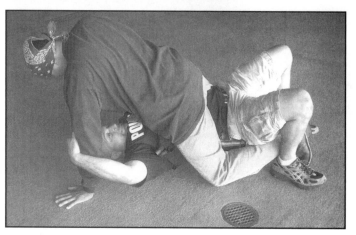

... buck your hips high and bridge onto your shoulders to...

...send him forward so that he posts his arm on the ground for balance. Quickly trap that arm and....

...roll him to that same side

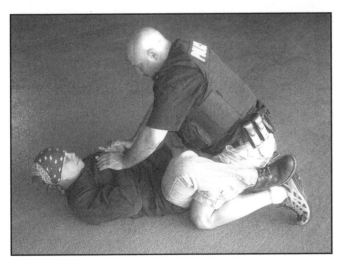

Roll up on top to establish control or scoot back and draw your weapon.

Simple sweep

The suspect attempts to choke you.

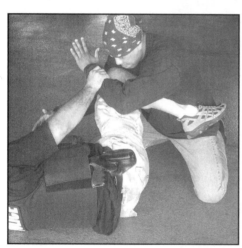

Clear your hips with hip escape by...

...placing one foot on the suspect's hip and the other outside of his knee.

Pull the suspect forward to off-balance him...

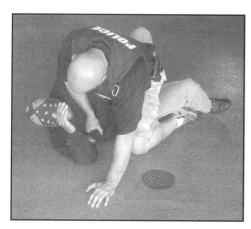

...and then scissor his legs to force him to roll onto his back.

The above defensive tactics illustrate basic principles of Brazilian jiu-jitsu, highly applicable techniques for law enforcement ground fighting. It's not enough to simply read through these; you must practice them and do so often.

Ground Kicking and Trapping

You're down, the suspect is standing and not running away. In fact, he still wants a piece of you. This isn't a good situation but it's not an impossible one. If he is advancing with a weapon, or his physicality or skill is superior to yours, you're justified in most jurisdictions to employ your weapon. Let's look at a few things you can do should you decide, for whatever reason, not to use it.

Trapping

For our purposes, trapping is any technique that prevents the suspect from moving his leg to avoid your offense.

Foot trap, leg hook

You're on your side with legs drawn in for protection as the suspect advances.

Trap his forward leg with your bottom ankle, shoot your other leg outward...

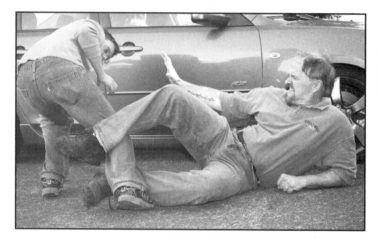

...and hook it hard behind his knee. He should go down, but if not...

...grab whatever you can to pull him down the rest of the way.

Foot trap, forearm press

You're on one or both knees. Trap his foot with one hand...

...and press your forearm into the side of his knee about two inches above his cap. Lean into it to buckle his leg.

Foot trap, shoulder ram

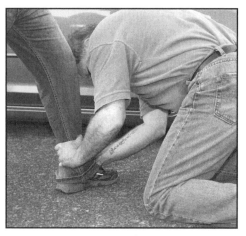

You're on one or both knees. Trap his foot with one or both hands...

...and slam your shoulder into the side of his knee.

Knee trap, foot pull

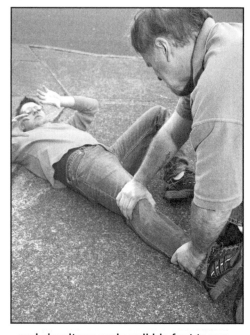

You're on one knee. Press into his kneecap...   ...and simultaneously pull his foot to you.

Don't lift his foot off the ground as you pull it toward you.
Do press firmly on his knee and pull/slide his foot toward you.

Kicking

Unless you're a trained kicker, your best targets are the suspect's knee, shin and groin. However, unlike in training when you get nailed in these targets, an adrenaline surge in a real fight often dulls pain. Therefore, don't stop after the first hit. Keep hitting until the suspect backs away and you can get up.

Groin kick

You're down and the suspect advances toward you. Draw your leg back...

...and slam your foot in.

If you have time, raise yourself and ram your hips forward as you kick.

Knee or shin kick

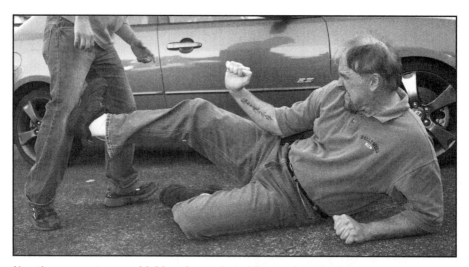

Use the same steps as kicking the groin to hit anywhere on his kneecap.

Practice these moves in the air, against a bag held by a training partner, and against an opponent with control. Make them part of your weapons cache.

Baton

What type of baton an officer favors is often determined by the amount of training time he's been given with it. The more time, the grater his skill, the more he likes it.

I carried a straight, light-weight metal baton for years, which I liked because I trained with it often and taught it to recruit academies. Then one day – after a controversial incident in which a suspect had died from an officer-applied sleeper hold - hundreds of side-handled batons arrived at our training unit. It was supposed to appease the officers after the front office banned the sleeper hold.

I hated the thing from the beginning because I found striking and thrusting with it to be an unnatural action under stress. My theory was that when you give a child a straight stick he swings it into your shin without any training. The side-handled baton, however, requires you to spin a little protrusion!

But since I had to teach it, I began to train with it – a lot. I practiced on my breaks, I took it home and practiced, and I made up an 18-count striking and thrusting set.

To my chagrin, I became quite proficient with it. Now, I still didn't like it but I could spin and thrust that thing like a real whiz bang.

Most other officers didn't like it either and with good reason: They received only two hours of training with it. So they complained long and hard until, a few years later, the front office bought everyone collapsible batons. Today, most don't like that one either.

In the end, you carry what you carry and, more times than not, you don't get a choice. Therefore, as long as you have to hang it from your belt, it's in your best interest to practice with it, and often.

Here are a few tips on ensuring that you're using the right body mechanics no matter what version you carry. The concept is simple:

Use improper body mechanics and your blow lands like a marshmallow.

Use the right body mechanics and you blow hits like a shotgun slug.

Body Mechanics

One day while training cops in an in-service class, I put on the Redman suit and faced a class of twenty officers who grinned as if just handed a free Starbucks. Why not? They were about to thump another cop who was dumb enough to let them do it.

If you haven't worn a padded suit, such as a Redman, imagine stumbling through Desert Valley, sun blazing at 130 degrees, while wearing clothing designed for Antarctica. It does a good job of absorbing most blows, though those that land in the thin places where the padded sections connect produce some serious stinging.

I shuffled about to give the trainees a moving target as one by one they advanced and whipped their collapsible batons into my legs, arms and ribs. Except for one or two who found the thin areas, the blows went mostly unfelt: then the instructor called for the line to hit me with two-handed thrusts.

With one hand near the front of the baton and the other near the end, the trainees, one after another, rammed their batons into my stomach and chest. Those I felt more than the strikes since the energy of a thrust is concentrated into the somewhat pointy end of the baton.

The next to the last trainee in line was a big SWAT man, a guy so huge they could have used him for their equipment van. With a gap-toothed, evil smile, he drove his baton into my solar plexus, knocking me back a step and sending a small, dull ache through the ol' breadbasket. Everyone laughed and patted the guy's tattooed muscles as he lumbered to the back of the line.

Last was a new officer, a man who weighed about 130 pounds, undoubtedly happy that the bureau no longer had a minimum height and weight requirement for hiring. I was still throwing good-natured insults at the SWAT monster when the little guy's thrust hit me like an artillery round, knocking me back several steps so that I had to desperately flail my arms not to fall over in the big suit. A wave of nausea swept through me that nearly brought up my lunchtime burger. I even looked down at my stomach to see if there might be a hole in the padding.

Later, after I'd removed the padded suit and rubbed my tender, soon-to-bruised stomach, I asked the small officer how he was able to hit me harder than all the others. I asked if he trained in the martial arts. He looked around to ensure no one was listening, and nodded.

When I asked him to demonstrate his form, it was immediately apparent how he was able to generate so much power. His body mechanics – hip snap, lead-leg lunge, speed, and obvious mental intent – were flawless. That was the difference that made him hit harder than even the oversized SWAT man who had hit me using only his muscles.

Martial arts legend, Bruce Lee, weighed about 135 pounds, but could hit with the same power as a 225-pound man. He once designed a heavy, hanging bag that not one of his training partners could move more than a few feet with their best punches and kicks. Lee could kick it so hard that it slammed into the ceiling.

Let's look at how you can incorporate proper body mechanics, as well as the suspect's momentum, to generate greater force with your collapsible baton, straight baton or side-handled baton.

STRENGTH

Strength matters. While this chapter is about ways to create force using precise body mechanics, strong muscles compound your power. You don't have to train like a bodybuilder; all you need are two, twenty-minute workouts a week to dramatically increase the strength in your legs, arms, chest and back. You will look better, feel better and, when you combine your new strength with proper body mechanics, your baton blows will land with awesome lethality.

Body mechanics

Common errors

- Trying too hard to compensate for weak muscles   You can actually make a technique weaker by trying too hard to make it stronger. When you put your all into a technique – body weight, balance and stability – you can easily overextend, lose your balance and fall into a pile. This usually gets a big laugh in training, but it can be disastrous on the street. The problem goes away once you learn how to control yourself and use good body mechanics.

- Fear and stress   These law enforcement bedfellows can cause you to put too much into a technique, thus making it weak, sloppy and inaccurate.

- Stiffness   This is often a byproduct of overcompensation and fear. It's also closely associated with a lack of good physical conditioning.

You can easily correct these negatives by getting into shape and by understanding that greater power comes from correct form and a little muscle. In that order.

Think hips

I remember my first karate teacher harping on the importance of twisting the hips when punching and kicking. "Eighty percent of your power comes from proper hip rotation," he repeated a thousand times. "Twist those hips!"

Now, I don't know where he got the 80 percent figure, but for sure incorporating the hips in your technique can be a primary factor as to whether your blow is powerful enough to stop a threat. When officers complained to me that their baton techniques hadn't worked on the street the night before, correct hip rotation was the most common missing element when they demonstrated their form.

The mechanics of hip rotation are simple. When you swing the baton to the right, your hips snap to the right. When you swing it to the left, your hips snap to the left. Those are the basics, but we're going to deviate from this classic martial arts approach and kick it up a notch to add even more power to the twist.

Straight or collapsible baton:

Say you're executing a right to left strike with your right hand.

You're swinging a baton from right to left.

Do strike through the target, allowing your hips to snap to the left. (right)

Don't stop your swing-strike on the target with your hips flush to the front, whether your target is a high one or a low one.

Side-handled baton:

You're swinging a side-handled baton from right to left.

Do strike all the way through, rotating your hips to your left. (right)

Don't stop your swing on the target with your hips flush to the front.

Straight thrust:

Don't thrust forward using only the power of your arm jab.

Do rotate your hips and turn your shoulder for more power.

Note 1: Be careful not to over rotate as it might cause you to do an awkward little spin and fall to the floor. Stop rotating just short of doing that.

Note 2: This over rotation doesn't work when doing a two-handed thrust, when your left hand grips near the front of the baton and your right hand grips near the butt. Instead, rotate your hips to the left until both are even to the front. It's difficult, if not impossible, to rotate them farther when gripping with both hands.

Think shoulders

It's important to incorporate your shoulders the same way you rotate your hips.

When striking right to left or thrusting with only your right hand, your shoulders should rotate past flush to the front until the side of your right shoulder is toward the target. When executing a two-handed thrust, however, your shoulders don't rotate past the flush-to-the-front position.

ROTATION

Don't let your shoulders rotate your hips, but rather let your hips turn your shoulders. To nitpick here, your hips should turn a hair of a second before your shoulders turn. However, if this small detail causes confusion or it's just too much to do, don't worry about it. Instead, just think about rotating your hips and your shoulders will automatically come along for the ride.

When applying a combination strike from right to left and left to right, snap your hips and rotate your shoulders on each pass.

Think heel

Traditional martial arts advocate that you maintain your rear foot flat on the ground. If you have been doing that, try a simple experiment. The next time you do a one- or-two-handed thrust, lift your heel and push off with the ball of your foot. I guarantee that you will immediately feel your power base increase.

Drive forward off the ball of your rear foot.

When you push a car out of a ditch, do you do it flat-footed? No, you push off the ball of your rear foot. The same is true when thrusting with your baton. In addition, when delivering strikes, your raised rear heel frees your body to turn with the blows, thus increasing your power.

Think abs

We all have an awesome six-pack of abdominal muscles, though too many donuts keep them hidden. Nonetheless, you can still tense them for a second upon impact.

Try this. Extend both of your arms about halfway out in front of you. Clench your fists as hard as you can while simultaneously making a short, deep-down-in-your-gut grunting sound. "Unnnggh!" Feel how your ab muscles tensed? Do the same thing when you hit with a baton.

Say you're doing a two-handed thrust. When the business end of your baton is about six inches away from the target (your muscles are only mildly tense up to this point), tense your arms and abdominal muscles as hard as you can. Martial artists call this focusing, an action that serves as a conduit to transfer power into the target. Making the "Unnnggh!" sound in conjunction with the tensing adds even more power.

Think speed

If you're new to baton training don't push for speed right away. If you try to be fast before your techniques are ready, your moves will likely be sloppy, weak and compromise your balance.

First, work to coordinate all the elements discussed so far. Once you feel that you're using your body mechanics properly, which can take four or five training sessions, you will see your speed developing naturally. Then and only then are you ready to push for greater velocity.

When I was writing *Speed Training: How to develop your maximum speed for the martial arts*, and five years later working on my DVD *Speed Training*, I happily found that I was getting faster simply because I was thinking about speed so much. When I interviewed several martial arts experts about speed and read what others had written about it, I found that they had discovered the same thing. A few of them even went so far as to say that 90 percent of being fast is to believe that you are fast.

It's important, therefore, that you have total conviction that you're already fast and that you're getting faster every training session. When you whip the baton into the bag, know deep in your mind that your strike is as fast as a lightening bolt. As you repetitiously thrust your baton in the air at an imaginary suspect, believe that you're moving at great speed.

Will this also work for speed drawing on the firing range? Yes.

Think momentum

For our purposes here, let's define momentum as the addition of your body weight into a strike and thrust. You can get this easily by stepping forward with your lead foot as you hit. Say you're standing with your left foot forward, holding the baton in a two-handed thrust position. Lunge forward with your lead foot, timing it so that the baton hits as your foot lands. So as not to slip, land on your heel first, and then set the rest of your foot down in a rolling fashion. Depending on the situation, your rear foot can immediately follow by scooting forward a few inches, or it can remain in place.

Use the Suspect to Increase Your Hitting Impact

Since the suspect isn't going to volunteer ways for you to hit him harder, you have to think up ways to trick him into doing so. Here are three:

Drawing

This martial arts trick adapts well to the police baton. When it works, which it does more times than it doesn't, try not to snicker. Here is how you can do it when hitting with a two-handed thrust, though it can be used with the strikes, too.

Say you're in that cliché dark, dank alley facing a huge suspect who has a tattoo of a pit bull on the side of his face. You're holding your collapsible baton in a two-handed grip as he dances around like a boxer. When you move toward him, he moves back, and he steps toward you when you step back. Ah-ha! You now have some good intelligence information: He's a follower.

Take a couple of short steps backward, your intent being to draw him toward you. When he advances...

... stop abruptly and explode forward with a thrust into his abdomen or chest. Combining your forward momentum and his multiplies the power of your blow.

Meeting his attack

The prerequisite for this one is that you have to be faster than the suspect. The idea is to meet his attack, perhaps his looping roundhouse punch, by stepping toward him and hitting him with a faster two-handed thrust. As with "drawing," you're generating more power because your momentum and the suspect's momentum come together. You must be fast (remember, believe that you're fast) or you're going to get clobbered.

A safer variation, though not quite as powerful, is to step diagonally forward, say to ten o'clock (the suspect is always at twelve o'clock) and simultaneously whip the baton in a one-handed strike across his closest leg. By moving off his straight line of attack, though still somewhat forward, you again combine momentums for greater power.

Break the circle

This isn't quite as powerful as the last two, but every little bit helps. Your baton is out and you're facing a threatening person who circles you, a common method of stalking that even trained fighters do. As he circles to your right, you move to your left in a circle to encourage him to keep moving in the same fashion. As long as you keep moving with him, he is always at twelve o'clock. Then when you stop but he keeps moving, he moves down the clock, which is what you want to add power to your baton strike.

You're circling to your left
as he circles to your right.

Just as he takes a particularly large or fast step toward two o'clock, you stop and whip your baton across his legs, waist, chest or closest arm. Your baton, arcing from right to left, meets his momentum as he moves into your strike.

When you train to incorporate proper body mechanics, you will feel the difference thrusting and striking the heavy bag within just a few days. If you're strong and already hitting the bag hard, but you aren't incorporating the right body mechanics, imagine how much stronger you will be when you do – and don't forget to trick the suspect into helping out, too.

Arresting Big Guys

"The bigger they are, the longer you're unconscious." - George Carlin

The biggest guy I've tangled with weighed 400 pounds and had been a weightlifting competitor in the Olympics. I'm guessing the heavyweight division. He was fat, he had giant muscles and he had the strength of the gods. The story was he had dropped a barbell on the back of his neck in competition, severely damaging a nerve there. From that day on, he experienced intense pain, made tolerable only by daily medications. One day he ran out of his meds and that's when a half dozen officers, including me, got a call on a "really big guy gone berserk and tearing up his house."

His hands were the size of Dodge Ram hoods and, for the first five minutes of our officer/citizen contact, he used them to toss us around his trashed living room while his mother hid behind a sofa on all fours calling out for us not to hurt her baby. Someone shouted "together, charge!" and we did, toppling him to the floor. Four of us draped our bodies over his four limbs and two more cops lay across his mountainous upper body. One smallish officer, who was clinging to a massive thigh, was tossed airborne. But to his credit, he courageously crawled back to straddle the limb again.

Handcuffs were out of the question and a pair of ankle restraints from an ambulance was too small. The two ambulance drivers got the idea to twist a couple of bed sheets into a "rope," which we used to bind the huge fellow's arms and legs.

Getting him onto a stretcher and stumbling with him on wobbly legs to the ambulance was not unlike the task the Egyptians had maneuvering those giant blocks of stone up the sides of the pyramids.

Facing a Big Suspect

If your sergeant asks, "Do you want to pull crosswalk duty at the grade school today, or do you want to serve this warrant on a sumo wrestler?" Choose the crosswalk gig.

Does Size Matter?

Yes…but not always (had you worried for a sec, huh?) If that's confusing it's because there are no absolutes when dealing with a big guy. Wrestling a person much larger than you can be your worse nightmare or it can be a piece of cake.

I know you have heard officers say, "Big guys are hard to take down," or "Defensive tactics techniques don't work on someone a lot larger than you." Or, conversely, "The guy was a giant but when I brought out the cuffs he turned into a whimpering mass of gelatin." Then there is the inevitable question we're discussing here: "How do you fight a really big guy, someone much larger and stronger than you?"

Many variables

There is no single, simple answer because there are no absolutes; it all depends on the individual suspect and the individual officer. The big guy might be an obese person who has never lifted a barbell or done a day of hard labor in his life. Or, he might be an obese guy who through trial and error has fought all challengers to win the All Kentucky Mountain Man Tough Guy Championships.

Maybe he is a steroid-soaked, 6' 6" bodybuilder, but because he is hardcore coward, he has never been in a fight in his life. Case in point: In my city, a skinny, short officer went to arrest a 6'4" professional bodybuilder who has flexed his oily stuff on the covers of bodybuilding magazines for years. But when the officer got to his house, the big guy cowered in the bathroom, refusing to come out, crying through the door that he was afraid the officer would bruise him. Of course, this doesn't mean you can be lax around these behemoths; there are many big pumpers out there who not only look good, but they can punch down a pillar at city hall.

What is the big guy doing at the moment of police contact? He might be offering passive resistance by simply sitting on a stool at the juice bar with his big guns crossed, saying, "I ain't leaving with you," or he might be charging at you using a full-sized pool table as a battering ram.

Then there's you. Your training, fitness level, experience, and mental outlook toward dealing with a big guy are important elements that influence the outcome of a physical arrest. If you have been deskbound for years and hate exercise, you will have a harder time than an officer who lifts weights, possesses polished defensive tactics, and has thought about ways to handle big guys.

What about pepper spray?

OC spray is certainly an option but, as you probably know, it doesn't always have the stopping power claimed in the advertisements.

- Worse case scenario – You spray him and he sucks it up as if it's his lunch and smiles appreciatively, "Mmm, pepper." Now you have to deal with a giant whom you've made hungry - and teary eyed.

- Best case scenario – He buries his face in his palms, bends over at the waist, drops to one knee, and moans, "Ma-ma."

So, with all these variables, how can you develop a plan of action when you're faced with a big fella who just ate your car? The answer is that you can't or, at least, you can't get specific. The good news is that you can train in a general fashion, you can talk about it with other officers, you can visualize scenarios, and you can develop a loose plan of action.

Mental preparation

A cop friend once got scooped up by a huge guy and cradled in the man's arms as if the guy were comforting a tired child after a long day at the circus. Except this "father" wasn't going to put him down. Instead of panicking, my friend crammed his thumb in the big ape's eye socket. His Hugeness dropped the officer unceremoniously onto the sidewalk and later filed a complaint for police brutality.

This technique might be frowned on by cop-watch groups, but for the officer being cuddled against his will, his simple defensive tactics move applied to this principle: A big guy might have a neck as big as the desk sergeant's belly, but he still has vulnerable targets, such as…

- eyes

- throat

- groin

- fingers

- shins

- toes

…body parts that don't like to be struck with a baton, sprayed with pepper, or gouged with a thumb.

Regard every person you arrest as dangerous and deal with them using the appropriate officer survival techniques. Maybe you consider drunks unpredictable; little guys to be quick; mentally deranged people to be impervious to pain; and big guys so strong they can slam dunk you into a dumpster.

While there is truth in these stereotypes, there are always exceptions and, if you have been on the job for a while, you know it's the exceptions you inevitably run into. There is the drunk who isn't unpredictable but he is the strongest person you have ever dealt with. There is the little guy who isn't fast at all but absorbs your hardest baton strikes with a smirk. There is that huge suspect who is as weak as your granny but is the fastest sprinter you've ever chased.

It's important to keep in mind that there are no absolutes when dealing with any person, no matter how large or small. Therefore, it's imperative that you go into every situation thinking and using your officer survival training to give yourself and your partners that all-important edge.

Preparation

You just stopped a tiny red sports car and out steps the largest man who ever wore jean overalls without a shirt. As your mouth drops open, the guy begins stomping toward you as if you were a free Las Vegas buffet. He wants you and he wants a big serving. Now is the time to put all of your training into play.

Here are some of the things that should be in your repertoire.

• **You've trained with big guys**   Just as you have practiced against an armed perpetrator, you should also practice all of you defensive tactics moves on a partner larger that you. If you're a big guy, practice as often as you can with other big guys. Know what it feels like to grab larger hands, bigger arms and contend with heavier mass. Know which techniques work well for you and which do not.

• **Understand joint locks**   Expect mixed results when applying joint locks.

> o It's common for big guys, especially those who have gotten big from weight training or hard, physical labor, to have a low tolerance to pain from joint locks. Maybe it's because their range of motion has been reduced by heavy lifting, thus making them more susceptible to having their muscles and tendons stretched.

> o Sometimes their great strength prevents you from maneuvering their limbs into position to apply a lock.

• **Have a Plan B**   Plan A is the first technique you apply. Plan B is the technique you change to when A falls apart on you. For example, you bend the big guy over with an armbar but he resists going all the way down. He eats the pain and begins to stand up. A common error is to struggle to make Plan A work, especially when the guy is bigger and stronger than you. Know that most grappling techniques require no more than 40 percent of your strength. So if you're applying 100 percent of your strength into the armbar and the suspect continues to overcome your hold – give it up and switch to Plan B, i.e., slam your palm into his chin and push him up and over in the direction he is moving.

• **Understand balance and leverage**   While it's always easier to deal with a big suspect on the ground where he has fewer options as to how he can move, it can be a problem getting him off balance enough to get him down there. Some big guys are rooted like a corner mailbox. On the plus side, once you get him off balance, he goes down hard, complete with a cloud of dust. Here are some ways to do that.

o Push his chin, his forehead or pull his hair in the direction you want him to go. This follows the principle: "Where the head goes the body follows."

o Use your knee or foot to press or slam behind his knee to buckle him. Whether he folds backward, forward or to one side, take advantage of it and push or pull him down in whatever direction he leans.

o Get him to overextend his weight by reaching toward you, so that he leans away or stumbles. Then apply a technique to help him fall in whatever direction he leans.

o Should you try to push him straight back from his front, he will simply step back with one foot and root himself. Instead, move in on him from a 45-degree angle. Use one or two hands, or your forearms, to push into his chest, upper arm or upper back at a slight upward angle. Pushing in shifts his weight back and pushing upward uproots him. This forces him to stumble in the direction you push him. Rush in before he can recover and take him down in the direction of his unbalance.

Some almost nevers

I'm using "almost" here because we must avoid absolutes. You can probably think of some exceptions to these "nevers" listed here and that's fine. That means you're thinking and analyzing. Always do that.

• **Never wait for him to attack you**   If your gut tells you that the big woman is going to resist, you need to go on the offensive. It's better for you to charge forward with speed and surprise than to wait to see what she is going to do. "Attack is the secret of defense." Some guy named Sun Tzu said that in *The Art of War*.

• **Never shake a big guy's hand**   Sure, it's good public relations to shake a citizen's hand. But it's not so good when he won't give your hand back and punches you with his other one.

• **Never let a big guy put his arm around you buddy like**   Seems like a no brainer but I've seen it happen. When a big guy wraps his arm around your shoulder it's an easy step for him to scoop up your legs with his other arm and carry you off into a forest.

• **Never let a big guy get close to you**   For that matter, never let anyone, no matter what size, get within arm's reach of you. It's just that a big guy can do that embarrassing pick-you-up thing.

Using your baton - targets

Say the situation has deteriorated to where you have to hit the big guy with your stick. Here are some target considerations:

• **Thrusting**   A thrust occurs when you ram the end of the baton into the target. You're concentrating all your energy into that one-inch diameter at the baton's end. Thrust into his chest, stomach and ribs. The below striking targets are too small to thrust at, especially in the heat of battle.

• **Striking**   A strike occurs when you swing the weapon into the target hitting with the side of the baton. His upper body and thighs are probably too cushioned with fat or muscle to feel your strikes. It's better to strike the fingers, back of the hands, shins and ankles.

Don't stay rooted when striking and thrusting a big guy. If he tolerates your first blows (always an unnerving moment), his next step may be to grab your baton, or you. Instead, hit and move. Thrust the baton into his abdomen and quickly step past him, whipping a hard strike into his calf or ankle. When he turns to reach toward you, move again as you strike his reaching fingers.

A psychological ploy

Here is a little trick that works sometimes. Keep in mind that a big criminal has stomped through his life using his bigness to intimidate others; therefore, he expects you to be intimidated or he is going to make an effort to ensure that you are. Play to his ego by saying something like, "Hey, you're too big to fight. You just might hurt me and I got a wife (husband) and kids." Or, "Wow, you're a big man. You ever thought about wrestling professionally?"

While it's always possible that the guy might try to prove you right, there is a greater possibility that your words will reduce his adrenaline. By recognizing what he has relied on so long to get through his sad life, he might drop his guard. When it works, his shoulders relax a little, tension leaves his face and his arms hang more casually.

That's when you charge in to take him down.

Here is another one you can try that worked for me... most of the time. The big guy threatens to thrash you. You say, "Okay, you can probably beat me to a pulp but then you have to beat up my backup officer. And then you'll have to beat up the next officer who comes, and the next. There are three hundred of us working tonight, not counting the state police and the FBI. You might get the first couple of us, because you are indeed a whopper of a man, but there will always be more of us coming. Pretty soon you're going to get tired and that's when we'll get you."

I've had big guys actually sputter out a laugh, and say, "Okay, you win. I'll go."

Now, if you work in a two-person department, this trick won't work.

BACK-UP

Police work isn't a contest. When the big guy says, "This is between you and me, copper," you must respond immediately.

"No it isn't. It's between you and the entire police department."

Don't look at the big guy as a challenge to your machismo, but see him as a problem, a problem that is best solved with a half dozen officers. Call them in and rush the guy from all angles.

Arresting a big guy can indeed be difficult, but just as you do with all problems that come your way on the job, you put into action the applicable concepts and principles from your training. Train for it and think about it ahead of time.

Training and Fighting Concepts

Let's look at a few concepts that pertain to dealing with dangerous people, to training, and to all-out fighting. As I've said a few times throughout this book, there are no absolutes in a fight; understanding this critical truth goes a long ways toward keeping your mug free of scars. Think about the concepts that follow and keep them in the forefront of your mind throughout your workday, and during the other 18 hours, too.

Concepts

Fighting concepts are just as important as techniques; some argue that they are more important given officers' limited training time. Think about the concepts here and ponder how they apply to what you do. Think about them in advance, so that they will serve you when your heart rate is going Mach 10 and your adrenaline is crashing against the rocks.

Survival Concepts

When justified to use force, don't hesitate

The late martial arts master Ed Parker said often, "Those who hesitate, meditate in the horizontal position…forever." He's right. In fact, hesitation to use force is one of the characteristics found in FBI research that gets cops killed. Keep in the forefront of your mind that force is justifiable in situations you reasonably perceive as threatening; you can even employ pre-emptive force to stop a threat. In other words, you don't have to wait until you're assaulted or injured. Besides, it might be too late to act then.

Don't quit

Don't give up because you're tired or injured. Author Kit Cessna – Delta Force veteran and SWAT officer – writes this in his excellent book *Equal or Greater Force*, published by Paladin Press:

"'It's never over until it's over.' When I was younger, I used to think that was just a quaint saying, but now I know that it is true. …it's meaning is simple. The fight isn't over until it is *really* over. Don't count yourself out; that's somebody else's job. If you find yourself in a situation where you are fighting for your very survival, then you don't stop for anything while you are still alive and moving. Plenty of people have received grievous injuries and gone on living. Plenty of people have gone into a fight where the odds appeared to be completely against them, yet they prevailed in the end. Many people have been in situations when they thought they were going to die, only to live and tell about it…Whatever you do, don't quit."

Don't take shortcuts

Sometimes it's the hard working, arrest driven officers who take shortcuts, shortcuts that get them hurt. I heard of one officer who did a quick pat down of a suspect, placed him in the backseat of the police car without handcuffing him, and then drove off to jail. Half way there, the officer realized he should have searched the man a little more thoroughly when he heard the distinctive sound of a round being chambered into to a shotgun. *His quick-search missed a great big shotgun!* The officer survived to tell the story.

Trusting your "cop's instinct" too much

You're a veteran cop and you can read people better than those with advanced psychology degrees. For sure, a cop's sixth sense about things is a powerful tool that even some courts of law respect. But, BUT, you just might be wrong next time.

 When I walked a beat in skid row I saw a cop get his jaw broken by an old wino he had arrested a dozen times before without incident. In fact, the officer had bought the man a meal on more than one occasion and had saved his bacon several times when other street folks wanted to kill him. This time after the officer picked him up out of the gutter and was walking him to the police car, the man shattered his face.

I once came this close to eating a big nail when I tried to scoot a street drunk out of the way so that tourists could make their way to a trendy shop. I had known this wino for 15 years and had never had a bit of trouble from him. This time he snatched a board with a protruding nail from his grocery cart and swung it at my head. My alert partner grabbed the man's arm and saved my skull from looking like a colander.

Your gut feelings are powerful tools, but don't count on them 100 percent. Don't count on anything 100 percent.

Philosopher Bertrand Russell said: "…fools and fanatics are always so certain of themselves, but wiser people so full of doubts." He also said: "I would never die for my beliefs because I might be wrong."

Training Concepts

Maybe we need to rethink the term "stance."

Every position is a fighting stance

Ask the average martial artist, boxer, high school wrestler, or one of those behemoth professional wrestlers to get into their fighting stance and each assumes a position in which their feet are staggered, their chin is tucked and their arms are configured in some sort of on-guard position. That's fine, but there are others, such as:

• sitting in your patrol car.

• sitting in a chair in the precinct interview room.

• standing in a city park with your foot on a tree stump.

• leaning against a wall sipping coffee.

• washing your hands in a restroom sink.

You have probably investigated assaults where the victim was sitting on a bus, using the men's room, leaning against a wall, sitting in a car, and so on. Well, these things happen to cops, too. An assault can explode at any time, anywhere, from any position you might be in.

As time permits, experiment with initiating techniques in this book from positions other than your standard feet staggered, arms up stance. Is it difficult to defend from them? Sure, which is why you need to practice. How well a real situation unfolds depends on how well you trained for it.

Practice from an arms crossed position:

Many officers like to fold their arms when talking with someone and that's fine. It's natural, non-threatening and just a tad less effective than the hands up and open position.

Don't wrap your arms in the standard folded arm position because you have to unwrap them to get them into play. That can take a second, too long.

Do drape or cup your hands on your upper forearms. They can snap into action must faster from this position.

Do use the one arm across the body and one arm up position. This one gets your hands into offensive and defensive action quick as a wink.

Do practice from these positions. Practice your blocks, grabs and strikes from whichever position you make your own.

Practice when you have a pen and notebook in hand:

Have you ever been jotting down a suspect's info when suddenly he goes berserk? Sure you have. Have you ever seen it happen to another officer and there was a big awkward moment when he didn't know what to do with his pen and notebook? Was that officer you?

Practice:

- blocking a push or punch when your hands are full.

- tossing the pen and notebook in your training partner's face.

- tossing them aside and counter attacking.

- slapping his face with a notebook and stabbing with the pen. (You will need another pen to justify the stab in your report.)

Distractions

Usually when you get into a physical confrontation with a suspect, you're yelling at him what's what, he's screaming back what's what, others around you are shouting what's what, and your police radio is calling your number to find out what's what. That's a lot of confusion to complicate your ability to function.

Here are some ways to train for it:

Practice talking while fighting:

Even when a technique, say a powerfully delivered armbar, gives clear direction to the suspect, it's important that you still verbally tell him what you want him to do. "Get down, get down, get down!" As discussed earlier, pain doesn't always give clear direction. Sure, it hurts him and he is jumping all about, but he isn't moving in a specific direction because the pain is vague. He doesn't know what he is supposed to do. Sometimes his confused reaction is so great that you give him more pain, but still the guy doesn't know what to do other than thrash about. Since in the heat of battle you might not remember which technique gives clear direction and which doesn't, play it safe and always provide verbal commands when training and on the street. "Get up, get up!" "Drop the knife, drop the knife!" "Sit down in the police car. Sit, sit, sit! Do it now!"

Practice talking while handcuffing:

Actually, this is something you can do when practicing any technique but it's especially hard when you're executing a relatively intricate handcuffing procedure. The drill is to talk about something, like fishing or mowing your lawn (in training, not with a real suspect). Talk to a third person about how to cook your favorite recipe as you handcuff your training partner in the prone position. When you can talk and cuff smoothly, you have arrived. Well, maybe you're not ready to do it in a biker bar as dozens of people scream for your scalp, but you're closer than if you always practice silently, concentrating on every minute step.

Form a crowd:

Practice handcuffing while other students crowd around you, catcall, and give you a hard time. The acting suspect should call you foul names and there should be police radios turned up full volume.

Note to instructors: It's not uncommon for the student acting as the officer to experience a blast of adrenaline during the crowd exercise. You need to caution that everyone use control so as not to hurt training partners. I have a bad shoulder today from overzealous trainees years ago.

Think about why techniques work

So many times students simply mimic the instructor. While they might do a good job of it, it's critical that they understand it. As you train in the academy or in precinct refresher courses, strive to understand why techniques work. You press here, and your training partner grimaces and comments on your mother. But why? Why did it hurt him? Why did he move in that direction and not this one? Why doesn't it hurt when you poke him here but he whines loudly when you poke a couple inches over?

Your job on the street is to ask who, what, when and why. In training, annoy your instructor with why questions. If he doesn't know, ask him to find out. Then you both know and you're both that much further ahead. Here is an example:

Consider the knee press discussed in Chapter 21

Trap the ankle and press your forearm against the inside of the leg a couple inches above the knee to...

...take him down.

By asking why it works, you understand that solidifying the suspect's ankle prevents him from escaping and it creates a base, and when you understand that pressing the vulnerable point a couple inches above his knee on the inside makes his leg buckle, you can make this technique work in a variety of ways and under a host of circumstances.

I show two in Chapter 21; here are four other ways that follow the concept:

1. Trap his ankle with one foot and press your other foot against the inside of his leg.

2. Use the curb to trap his foot and press his leg with whatever best fits the moment.

3. During the scuffle, your partner's foot inadvertently traps the suspect's foot. Seize the moment and push his leg with whatever is available to you.

4. Trap his foot with your hand and slam your head into his leg.

There are more. See if you can discover them now that you understand "the why," the elements. Do this with all your techniques.

Out of the Norm Handcuffing Concepts

Sure, you can handcuff and apply your other tactics using two healthy hands, but what if you're in a situation in which you can only use one? You don't know? Better practice so that you do know.

Practice handcuffing with one hand

You've been brawling with the brute all by yourself for five minutes and you finally get him down on the ground and semi controlled. He is squirming and wanting to get up and you're managing to control him with your one uninjured hand. Now you have to cuff him. Can you do it with one hand? Maybe, but for sure you can do it more smoothly if you practice it in advance. How are you going to control his free hand as you handcuff the other? Pin it with your knee? Your chest? Your hip? Sit on it? These are all possibilities given the particulars of the situation. Practice it now.

Practice fighting with an injured limb

I devoted a chapter to this in *Fighter's Fact Book 2,* also published by Turtle Press, so I'll just mention its importance briefly. Suffering an injury in a scuffle comes with the territory. You jam a finger, tweak your wrist, bang your knee and strain your gizzard. But since you're getting paid the big bucks, you can't stop. If the injury is especially intense, you have to function with one arm, one hand, or while hopping on one leg.

By practicing in advance, you dramatically increase the odds of doing this well while being mindful of officer safety. Your ability to execute takedowns, control holds and restraints is highly dependent on prior practice and your understanding of why techniques work.

Fighting Concepts

Action/reaction

Action is faster than reaction, or to say it another way: reaction is slower than action.

Never let a suspect, even a complainant, get within touching range unless you're going to make a hands-on arrest. No matter how skillful you are and no matter how intoxicated, mentally deranged, or infirm the suspect might be, if he throws a sucker strike without telegraphing, you're likely to get struck. By the time you see a punch, push or kick coming at you, he has already decided to attack and set his thought into motion. That puts you in a position of having to play catch-up and 99 times out of 100, your reaction will be too late. Should his attack be with a hammer or a goldfish bowl, you're a goner.

"Open the door" with speed

The situation has reached a point where you must hit the suspect with your arms legs, or a baton. Should your first hit be fast or hard? This is an often-debated question among martial artists. My belief is that you should open the door with speed. Get inside quickly with that initial baton thrust or palm-heel strike and then follow with harder blows.

Go for his right arm

Since most people are right handed (statistics say 70 to 95 percent), it makes sense to grab a suspect by his right arm. This can have a powerful psychological effect on the person as well as limit his physical response. That said, it might not have any effect at all so don't count on it. Still, grab his right arm whenever you have the option.

Training tip: Make sure you practice your control holds equally on your training partner's right and left side.

Stand on a curb or step

Do this to appear larger to the suspect. It works, but has its risks, especially if the suspect pushes you and there are other steps above yours to trip you.

Drop-step for power

This is amazingly effective and especially valuable when in close. It's a favorite concept among boxers and more and more martial artists are discovering its power, too.

Don't pick your lead foot up in the air.

Do lift your weight off it ever so slightly and then drop your weight onto it hard as your palm-heel strike or baton thrusts lands.

Hit his hand

The human hand is easy to hurt and the pain can be quite acute. This was a favorite technique of mine and the result was always the same: the suspect would jerk his pained hand back toward himself, usually against his body, and reach for it with his other hand. Then, while he was preoccupied with all that, I moved in on him.

The suspect begins to advance.

Strike the back of his hand (lots of nerves there that hate to be struck) or his fingers.

Create good witnesses

When you tell your suspect what to do, it not only gives him clear direction and reduces the chance of you having to use greater force, it also lets witnesses see what you are trying to accomplish. As you well know, witnesses perceive what their experiences (or lack there of) and prejudices (good and bad) allow them to see. When you give clear commands to the suspect, you provide witnesses a clearer picture. Of course, there will always be those who see what they want to see.

When I worked downtown where every little arrest would draw a crowd, one of us would go over to the onlookers after we had stuffed the suspect in the backseat, and apologize for the situation and the suspect's resistance, explaining in general terms the reason for the arrest. Most often we received a scattering of "thank you officer" and the folks went on about their day.

Three good targets

When other techniques have failed and you're justified to use extreme force, consider these three last resort targets.

- **Eyes:** If the suspect can't see it's hard for him to stab, shoot or bludgeon you. You can 1) rake your fingers across his eyes like a windshield wiper, 2) you can poke, a la The Three Stooges, or 3) or you can ram your fingers in hard and deep.

- **Throat:** A hard punch, chop, elbow strike, forearm slam or baton strike to the front of the neck will stop even the toughest adversary.

- **Shins:** A hardened bouncer told me that a hard kick to a person's shins has never failed him. Only a thin layer of skin covers most shinbones and their tender nerves. Slam your hard shoe or boot into the suspect's shin and then rush in and clothesline him to the ground.

Drive him backwards

You can move forward faster than he can back up. When he retreats defensively from you, charge him hard and fast to confuse his thinking and overpower him physically.

High/low

When striking with your baton, hit his elbow and follow with a blow to his shin. Then hit his elbow again. Hitting high then low, or low then high, disrupts the brain. I have found that the recipient's clear thinking shuts down around the fourth or fifth blow.

Concepts to take on patrol

1. **Action is faster than reaction**. I have had countless officers tell me over the years that remembering this concept saved them on the street.

2. **You can't judge how dangerous a suspect is by his appearance**. Even dweebs can pack a weapon or know kung fu.

3. **Always watch the suspect's hands**. If you can't see one of his hands, be very concerned.

4. **You can see every action a suspect makes by watching the triangle formed by his chin and shoulders**. Continuously move your eyes from his eyes to his shoulders.

5. **Execute your attack** – body-weapon hit, joint lock or baton strike – with authority so that the suspect isn't given an opportunity to strike back.

6. **Be cognizant of the suspect's friends**. When making a physical arrest, position yourself so you can watch his buddies.

7. **Stay alert**. See everything.